Via Publishing

9039 Sligo Creek Pkwy, Silver Spring, MD 20901

www.plamenpress.com

Copyright © Rachel Miranda Feingold, 2021

Via Publishing 2021

Printed in the United States of America

10 9 8 7 6 5 4 3 2 1

LIBRARY OF CONGRESS CATALOGING-IN-PUBLICATION DATA

Miranda, Rachel

The World at Our Table: A Euro-American Cookbook of Family Favorites/Rachel Miranda

ISBN: 978-1-951508-04-3

Library of Congress Control Number: 2015935563

Illustrations © Serena Faye Feingold 2021

Cover design by Serena Faye Feingold

THE WORLD AT OUR TABLE

A EURO-AMERICAN COOKBOOK OF FAMILY FAVORITES

Happy cooking!

Rachel Miranda

Serena Faye Ferguson

THE WORLD AT OUR TABLE

A EURO-AMERICAN COOKBOOK
OF FAMILY FAVORITES

RACHEL MIRANDA

ILLUSTRATED BY SERENA FAYE FEINGOLD

Via Publishing

"What are you eating?" Dad (David) asks.
"Raisins…" says Gabriella, spaced out.
"What are you thinking about?" says Dad.
"Nothing."
"You mean there's nothing at all that you're thinking about…?"
"Nuh uh."
"Take out the little computer in your mind and tell me what's in it."
"All that's in it is…raisins!"

Jacob taps his fingers on the table. "Is it time for brownie pudding yet?"
"Not yet, sweetie. We have to have dinner first," says Mom (Rachel).
"But when is that going to be?"
"Soon, Jakey," Mom says. "I promise."
"But the brownie pudding is already done?"
"Yes! All done."
"Well then, can we have brownie pudding for dinner?"

In her second and third years, Serena subsists on noodles, orange juice, pretzels, and cheese.
But mostly noodles, or "noonies" in Serena-language.
Mom asks, "Why do you love noodles so much, Serena bean?"
"Noonies are good!" Huge grin.
"It's true. They *are* good!" says Mom. "But why do you love them?"
"*You* have some. Okay, Mama?" Nods expectantly.
Mom laughs. "Okay, Bean."
Serena will redefine her four food groups again and again—but noodles always remain.

Jesse in fifth grade:
"What are you going to demonstrate for us, Jesse?" asks Mrs. Christopherson.
"I'm going to make crème brûlée."
"Really? But that's going to be very complicated!"
"I know!" Excited smile. "Is it okay if I bring my mini blowtorch to school?"

To my four spectacular children, Gabriella, Jake, Serena, and Jesse,
and my two extraordinary kids-in-law, Louis and Mayu.
In celebration of Gabriella and Louis's wedding,
Jake and Mayu's marriage,
and the arrival of my delicious grandson, Asher Meir,
the first baby of our next generation.

 CONTENTS

COOKING TIPS TO LIVE BY: PREHEATING POTS; HEAVY-BOTTOM PANS

THE IMPORTANCE OF SALT; COOK AHEAD

ENTRÉES

INTRODUCTION:
SHARING OUR TABLE

Cooking for family and friends has been a passion of mine since I was a small girl growing up in Switzerland, where my American parents had been living and working since 1960. My first love was baking cakes. I derived deep satisfaction from offering little treats to my Swiss schoolmates and my parents' ex-pat friends; it gave me a feeling of being anchored in the space between these communities, though I didn't really belong in either. When I was eight, my parents decided it was time for our family to return to America, a place where my siblings and I had never lived. I imagined that in this land where anyone could belong, I would find the roots I had been searching for.

The reality was nothing like I had envisioned. Our foreign accents did not win us any welcoming smiles in the small New England town my parents chose, and to complicate things further, we were one of only a handful of Jewish families in the area. Those early immigrant years left me wondering if I would ever find a sense of belonging. But over time, these few Jewish families became a tight-knit group that gathered regularly for Shabbat dinners, and eventually founded the first synagogue on the Connecticut shoreline, giving me my first glimpse of a deeper rootedness that had nothing to do with place. As a teenager and all through college, I became increasingly attached to the Jewish traditions, and especially to food-centered rituals, the festive meals that required careful planning and preparation so they could take place in a sacred time set aside just for them.

I married right out of college, eager to make a home where I could find my own way of expressing the Jewish heritage that I shared with my husband, David. We had four kids in six years, and in the beautiful chaos that followed, I held fast to the weekly rhythm of Shabbat, cooking ever-larger meals in the hours before sundown on Friday, and inviting friends to partake of them with us. Despite the challenges of maintaining a kosher kitchen, I was always striving to expand my skills as a cook.

Over the next twenty-five years, we logged an epic number of meals together. Our Shabbat table grew and grew; droves of our children's friends came for lunch every Saturday, and my parents became a regular fixture as well. Sometimes it seemed as though the whole neighborhood was at our table, saying with a grin, "I've come for the warm challah," or, "We heard you were making your squash pie."

As the kids got older and the chaos abated, I found time to take a more nuanced look at my cooking practices: Why did a humid day doom my meringues to fail? Why did the balance of colors and textures on a plate matter? I started to notice differences between my food and "typical American" cooking, if there is such a thing. For instance, I had always felt that most desserts in this country

were too sweet for me, but I hadn't considered the fact that this was a learned preference: European recipes simply use less sugar. I began to read cookbooks more closely; I devoured chefs' memoirs and watched TV cooking channels. I became more ambitious, and some of my dishes grew elaborate and time-consuming. Often, I got ahead of myself and tried to learn or do too many things at once. But sometimes things went brilliantly, and we all delighted in the results.

All of my kids participated in these culinary adventures from time to time, and their tastes and interests kept the engine of my kitchen humming. When my youngest, Jesse, was just four years old, he began to cook with me on a regular basis, and his curiosity and mischief allowed me to become more playful with my cooking. Jesse's culinary ambitions grew as he did, and by the time he was in high school, he had mastered crème brûlée and even catered a party or two. He went on to earn a degree in culinary arts, and his joy in cooking has multiplied my own. A couple of his recipes are in this book, and his fingerprints are on lots more.

In time, the children began leaving the nest, and eventually, David and I also went our separate ways. I sought comfort in building new friendships in the creative writing community, and before long, found a way to bring my writing friends and my faraway kids to the table with me, by posting elaborate descriptions of my weekly Shabbat menus on Facebook. When I moved to Washington, DC, I also moved away from my religious lifestyle—but I kept the practice of making Shabbat dinner every week. In the lively and diverse community where I found myself, these meals became quite literally a global experience; I happily cooked for new friends from Bangladesh, Libya, the Czech Republic, Japan, Spain, Canada, and India. The world at my table. I loved it.

This shift in my life brought me a deeper perspective on my own ancestral history: I came to see that the homes we make for ourselves are inextricably bound up with our origin stories, however fraught they might be, and the food we cook and share helps us to keep those connections alive.

I began working on this cookbook in 2014 as a wedding gift for my oldest daughter, Gabriella. Life had other plans for me, though, and I found myself still revising in early 2020. As winter turned to spring, I was finally nearing the finish line when the world was tilted off its axis by the weight of two words—*novel coronavirus*—and everything changed.

Writing a cookbook during a global pandemic has felt both absurd and utterly, undeniably right: Somewhere in the midst of the fear, the surrealism, and the isolation, I realized that my relationship to food and the very act of cooking for others had shifted forever. The book that has emerged out of this time is not the same as the one I started.

Worries about food supply and scarcity in this pandemic-altered landscape made me want to know the provenance of the food I was making: where on this earth was it first grown? How did it

travel to other parts of the world to begin with, and how was it getting to me now? Which peoples and cultures first put together a particular combination of flavors, and what was happening around them at the time? Investigating these global questions also led me to examine again my attachment to certain flavors and dishes. Why, exactly, were they meaningful to me? In writing out my recipes, I saw that they reflected my struggle to amalgamate my European and American selves, my Jewish and universally spiritual selves. How could I hold onto a sense of belonging while remaining in those liminal spaces?

The answer was there in the food itself. Cooking for those I love is how I create that sense of belonging; how I connect those disparate parts of myself. Knowing that the recipes alone could not convey the meaning of these connections, I have paired them with the food origin stories, personal reminiscences, and family anecdotes about what makes them especially beloved.

Of course, the recipes tell their own stories, too. When I was young, we went on yearly family vacations in Italy, which was only a few hours' drive from Zurich but might as well have been worlds away. The passion and emotional generosity that infuses every part of Italian culture, that is woven into the bright, sunny colors and flavors of the food, went right to my heart and stayed there. My abiding love for all things Italian—for the fragrant lemons and almonds, the juicy tomatoes, garlic, basil, and the sharp nuttiness of Parmigiano Reggiano—is reflected in many of the recipes you will find in this book, from Italian Wedding Soup to Pasta Puttanesca to Torta Caprese.

The farm-centered cuisine of Switzerland is highlighted here as well, in dishes like Farm Eggs, Muesli, Tomato Bisque, and Creamy Vegetable Curry—foods I loved as a child and made for my own children. The French culinary tradition has also impacted my cooking, showing up in recipes like Zucchini Vichyssoise and Haricots Verts with Toasted Onions, along with the tarts, custards, and floral flavors of apricot and raspberry that are ubiquitous in the desserts of Western Europe. In turn, these influences have mingled with flavors native to the Americas, in such dishes as Summer Corn Tart, Agave Lime Salmon with Honeydew Salsa, and Grilled Pineapple with Cinnamon Crème Fraiche.

My continental affinities are rounded out by the Eastern European specialties of my ancestors, foods of the *shtetl* to which I was mysteriously attracted before I had ever tasted them: kugels and knishes, stuffed cabbage and kasha varnishkes. This last one, a favorite dish of my parents, mingles buckwheat groats and bow tie pasta with caramelized onions and chicken fat to marvelous effect. My father—who my kids and I called Poppi, and who died last year while I was working on this book— was a very particular eater, but he used to rhapsodize about the knishes in Brighton Beach; I even had a chance to taste one just after we arrived in America, while my father's own father was still alive. My connection to these old-world flavors and customs is indelibly woven into my recipes.

A new sense of the sacred has entered my cooking life as I've learned to consider its global context. Since my recipes have grown organically out of my personal experiences with food, by default

this is both a kosher cookbook and one of ecological-culinary activism. You won't find any dishes here that combine meat and dairy, or any recipes calling for pork or shellfish. What you will find is a large selection of vegetarian dishes and a creative use of dairy alternatives and plant-based ingredients that responds directly to our present-day interests. As a culture, we are coming to see that our relationship with the earth is inseparable from the food we buy and make to nourish our families. I am trying to seek out as many locally grown and naturally sourced ingredients as I can find and afford: grass-fed beef and free-range chicken and eggs, local dairy, seasonal produce, and whole, unprocessed grains.

These days, it often feels impossible to think about making beautiful food, much less to worry about where it comes from, when people are dying from a pandemic and it seems that nothing will ever be the same again. But in fact, being homebound for months on end, and under such dire circumstances, has pushed us to turn inward, both emotionally and logistically. We have returned to our kitchens in historic numbers; and we are confronted with daily evidence that we must start considering the needs of the earth along with our own. These are unexpectedly positive outcomes of household quarantine—ones I hope will stick long after this bleak time has become a distant memory.

I believe that something essential is lost when we do not prepare our own food and sit down to eat it together. I have made it a priority during the many, many times I've moved houses in my life—between Zurich neighborhoods when I was a small child, then across the Atlantic and around New England, and then, as a young mother and the wife of a physician-in-training, from the northeast to the Midwest to the Deep South and back again; even in midlife, my neighborhood has continued to change. That was not what I had planned. I always thought I would have to put down permanent roots to really know belonging. But wherever I find myself, even in the midst of chaos and uncertainty, I feel instantly more at home after I've cooked that first meal—usually a simple pasta dish—and cleared a space on the table to share it with whoever is in my household.

I am aware that the idea of making fresh and beautiful food is a privileged concept. I know that not everyone can avoid eating processed foods, or access "the freshest lemons" and "local dairy," as I often enjoin you to do in these pages. Countless people are cut off from such options.

That said, if you have a kitchen, and a bit of energy, it is worthwhile to cook whatever real food you can for yourself and your family. The nutritional payoff from cooking at home can't be overstated. If fresh fruits and vegetables are not available to you, frozen or canned will often substitute. The upshot is this: any food that is recognizably close to its original form is preferable to processed squares and triangles.

While some of the recipes in this book are elaborate or time-consuming and might appear out of reach if you are not a practiced cook or don't have easy access to ingredients, I have tried to offer

suggestions for short-cuts and substitutions wherever possible; I recommend you start with a simple soup or pasta dish, and work your way up. And if you have the time and opportunity to play a bit in the kitchen, I hope you will tune in to some deeper questions: What is your body craving? What foods are in season, and how can you adjust a recipe you're excited about to accommodate what's fresh now? What flavors complement each other, and which ones tend to crowd each other out? What feelings, memories, dreams arise when you smell or taste certain foods? How do members of your family—however it is configured—respond to the food you have made for them?

Above all, I hope you will find ways to eat with your family and friends—if possible, around some sort of table—and ideally, with phones and other screens stowed away for the brief time it takes to consume the food you have worked so hard to put there. When my kids were teenagers and personal cell phones were just becoming a thing, we made an effort to leave them out of the room during mealtimes. And then, in those years, Shabbat gave us all a twenty-five-hour weekly break from using screens, a golden opportunity to connect on a deeper level. Setting aside any religious considerations, I believe that everyone can benefit from such a practice. The simplest of meals eaten face-to-face, without those ever-present screens to pull our focus away, allows connections to unfold: conversations, arguments, songs, laughter, grievances, longings, and even the occasional revelation. In the end, all of it keeps us closer to one another.

It's been several years now since all of my children have grown and scattered. My sense of belonging has shifted and shifted again with each configuration, and the definition of what it means to invite the world to my table has changed as well. Through it all, our family remains fiercely close, a fact that has never felt more important than it does now—and that I believe is due, in large part, to our years of sharing meals at the same table. When we are able to come together these days, it's still, always, around "the table," even if the coronavirus pandemic has compelled us to reimagine how we define that, too—by sharing dishes between households or by getting creative with the seating. Recently, we gathered for a ceremony to mark the first anniversary of my Poppi's death, and to share a family meal while spread out at a safe distance from each other under the trees in my backyard. The presence there of my dear little grandson, Asher, wreaking havoc with the tablecloth and burbling his delight at the blueberries and the birds, manifested our hopes for a brighter future as we discovered the world again through his wonder-filled eyes.

I am so very grateful to my younger daughter, Serena, for her loving hours and months of labor in making the illustrations for this book. I hope that they, combined with these origin stories and family recipes, will help nurture in you a love of food that you will pass down to your children's children as I will to mine. May we all continue to break bread together for many generations to come.

COOKING TIPS TO LIVE BY

YOUR KITCHEN AS A MICROCOSM

Modern life is busy, and we are constantly being pulled in a hundred directions. But we all have to eat. If you're thinking about cooking more often, you might find it helpful to envision your home kitchen as a microcosm of restaurant culture: while the chef is the central driving force, others in the kitchen learn from the master and take turns preparing aspects of the menu themselves. There is usually a whole team working together—sous-chefs, prep cooks, line cooks, busboys, and dishwashers. Other members of your household or community can take on some of these roles, as helpers and collaborators. Inviting them to do so will foster a communal atmosphere in your kitchen, and might just leave you with the energy and good humor to enjoy the food you make.

**More Cooking Tips to Live By
can be found throughout this book.**

BREADS

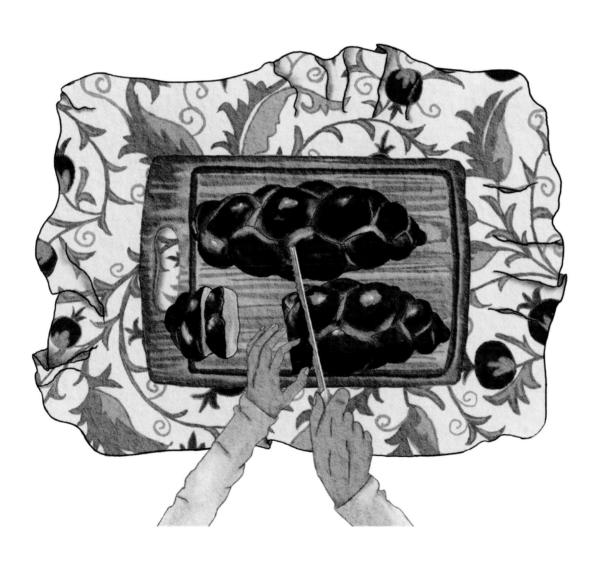

FAVORITE CHALLAH

Breaking bread is as elemental to Jewish tradition as the Torah itself. The word *challah* in biblical Hebrew simply means loaf or cake, and from the earliest mention of manna as a special "loaf" that fell from heaven to feed those who wandered in the desert after the Exodus from Egypt, bread became inextricably bound up in mealtime rituals that have been carried on through millennia and continue to this day.

I started making my own challah when my children were very young and there was barely time for showers, much less yeast breads. I had never attempted a yeast bread before, but during that time, I made a new friend who had just as many kids as I did, and she was making challah every week. I thought her practice was simply crazy until the first time she offered me a taste. Then something shifted in me. Once I had figured out the recipe I liked best, I would make half a dozen loaves at a time, freezing three so I only had to make it every other week. Like any habit, after a while it became part of my routine. I could never go back to store-bought. My recipe is a lot like a French brioche, smooth, eggy, and somewhat sweet, in keeping with Ashkenazi tradition—though I have suggested a lovely multigrain alternative that adds a more Sephardic texture. You will also see that the recipe calls for margarine: because kosher laws prohibit mixing meat and dairy in the same meal, and the festive Sabbath meals traditionally include meat, challah recipes are most often *pareve* (the Yiddish word for neither meat nor dairy). But butter works fine here, too.

When my kids were growing up, we observed the traditions around breaking bread for the many hundreds of Shabbat meals we shared together. The loaves of challah sat under a special cloth, untouched until everyone completed the ritual handwashing. An anticipatory silence would spread around the table as each person finished washing and waited, without speaking, for the others to do the same, a tradition meant to help participants maintain a singular focus on the blessing over the bread. But somehow, in our house, we could never stay silent for long enough, so we would hum an old Jewish folk tune, drumming on the table with our hands until the last person was seated. After blessing the bread, we would sprinkle it with salt—or at Rosh Hashanah, with honey for a sweet new year—and tear pieces from the warm loaves, sighing with pleasure as we took that first bite.

You will need several hours from start to finish for this recipe, including breaks for first and second risings. The order of the steps is important here, so I have numbered the instructions below.

2 c. warm (not hot) water
3 Tbsp. active dry yeast
2 Tbsp. raw sugar
9½ c. unbleached flour (or see multigrain option below)*
1 c. raw sugar
1 rounded Tbsp. salt
1 c. margarine, pref. Earth Balance® (or butter)
4 eggs, slightly beaten
1 tsp. neutral oil (canola or vegetable)
Sesame or poppy seeds, or yellow raisins, if desired
1 beaten egg, mixed with 1 Tbsp. water, for egg wash

*For a nutty multigrain loaf, replace 2 c. all-purpose flour with 2 c. whole wheat flour plus 2 Tbsp. flaxmeal.

1. Place warm water in a small bowl. Sprinkle on yeast and 2 Tbsp. sugar. Stir briefly and allow to bubble. (If no bubbles form after 10 minutes, the yeast is dead; you'll need a new batch so the bread will rise.)

2. In a large bowl, mingle flour (and flaxseed meal, if desired), sugar, and salt. Cut margarine into chunks and add to flour mixture, working it all together gently with your hands until it looks like clumpy dirt.

3. Beat eggs briefly, and add them and the warm yeast mixture (should be bubbly) to the large bowl. Mix with your hands just until dough holds together.

4. Create a clean, flat surface to work on, and turn dough onto it. Use hands to knead the mixture until it is integrated. If it is sticking to your fingers or your counter, add small handfuls of flour up to about another ½ c., until dough is no longer tacky but elastic and smooth, only leaving the barest residue on your hands.

5. Oil a very large bowl with canola or vegetable oil. Roll the dough into a big ball, place in the oiled bowl, turn over once to coat, and cover with a clean dishcloth. Set in a warm place (like on top of the stove with the oven set on low) and rise for 60 to 90 minutes until dough doubles in size.

6. Turn dough out onto a clean surface and punch it down (this is the fun part—literally punch the air out of the dough!), then knead briefly until most of the bubbles have gone out. If you want raisins in some or all of your challah, this is the time to work them in (use about 2 to 4 Tbsp. per loaf).

7. Divide dough into 5 or 6 mid-size chunks, dividing those chunks into 3 pieces each and using your hands to roll them into round strands. Braid the strands, making sure ends are well pinched together. You can also make this recipe in 3 or 4 eight-inch cake pans as pull-apart loaves: Instead of strands, roll dough into small balls, and place 5 of them in a circle around the edges of each pan, placing a sixth ball of dough in the center. When they rise again (see step 8 below), they will merge together to create pull-apart loaves.

8. Place braided loaves on greased baking pans, with no more than two on a pan so that they won't flow together when they rise again. (Pull-aparts remain in cake pans.) Cover dough with clean cloth and let rise for another hour or two in a warm spot, until they look rounder and considerably bigger than before.

9. Preheat oven to 325 degrees. Remove cloth and brush loaves with egg wash (1 egg mixed with 1 Tbsp. water) using a pastry brush. If you want to add sesame or poppy seeds, sprinkle them on after egg wash.

10. Bake for 20-25 minutes, switching racks halfway through, so loaves brown evenly. They are done when the loaves are golden brown. If you have doubts, turn one over with a dish towel and knock gently, listening for a dull sound. Remove from oven and allow to cool for 10 minutes before moving.

Serve warm. Or cool completely and wrap each loaf in foil to freeze any challah you are not using in the next 24 hours. To serve, warm in foil directly from freezer in a 350-degree oven for 10 to 15 minutes or in a 200-degree oven for up to one hour. Leave in foil to keep warm until ready to serve.

This challah is superb on its own, but it is extra delectable with a drizzle of honey. *Makes 5 to 6 medium braided loaves or 3 to 4 pull-apart round loaves.*

HONEY CORNBREAD

Cornbread was a favorite of my Poppi's, and he liked it on the sweet side. Though my parents only ever bought a handful of packaged or prepared foods, I still remember the smell of Thomas's Corn Toast-R-Cakes toasting for his breakfast. Maybe that's where my nostalgia for cornbread comes from. Or maybe it's the sunny, warm smell and cheery color, which can take the edge off even the iciest winter's day.

Corn, called *maize* in many cultures, is native to the Americas, and was first cultivated over seven thousand years ago in what is now Mexico. Cornmeal is made by grinding the kernels—traditionally with stones, or in modern processing, with steel rollers—into varying degrees of coarseness to make hundreds of different dishes. Stone-ground cornmeal is the most nutritious kind, because the corn's hull and germ have not all been filtered out; unfortunately, it comes at a premium in the US, where it is routinely processed and stripped of most of these nutrients. You might have to go out of your way to find stone-ground cornmeal, but I recommend it. Besides offering you more nutrients, it will yield a more interesting bread.

1 c. yellow cornmeal, pref. stone-ground
1 c. unbleached all-purpose flour
1 Tbsp. baking powder
½ tsp. salt
¼ c. honey (or more to taste)
¾ c. milk (or nondairy substitute)
2 eggs, beaten
¼ c. neutral oil (like Canola or sunflower)

Preheat oven to 400 degrees. Combine dry ingredients in a bowl. Make a well or indentation, and add wet ingredients, stirring briefly with a fork between additions until just blended. Pour into an 8 x 8-inch baking pan or 12 muffin cups. Bake only 20 to 25 minutes for pan, or 12 to 15 minutes for muffins, until set. Moist crumb should still be visible on the tester. Don't overbake! It will quickly become dry and crumbly.

This cornbread always features on our Thanksgiving table as a first course, often alongside Summer-Winter Soup. (See Whole Berry Cranberry Sauce and Pecan Pie for thoughts about the Thanksgiving holiday.) It is also delicious as a snack with a slice of cheddar, or my personal favorite—for breakfast, still warm, with butter and raspberry jam. *Makes about 16 squares.*

GOLDEN ZUCCHINI BREAD

I've been making zucchini bread for so long that I can't even remember when it started. The smell of cinnamon would draw my children to the kitchen with dreamy eyes; they loved to break into the mini-muffins, never suspecting that something so sweet could have veggies in it.

Over time, I played around with my recipe to see if I could sneak even more nutrients in. I was delighted that substituting whole wheat for some of the white flour and adding a couple of tablespoons of flaxseed meal only made it tastier. The texture was still just as moist, but it had a distinct nutty flavor. I cut out half of the sugar and no one missed it. I discovered Vietnamese cinnamon, which has a stronger flavor than other varieties due to its high concentration of essential oils, and that got thrown in there, too. I also found that with only a couple of substitutions, I had a whole new variation: pumpkin chocolate chip (see below). When the kids got older, I sometimes added walnuts. The turmeric came last, boosting the cinnamon's anti-inflammatory properties and adding a slight golden hue to the cake. By now, this little recipe is so full of nutrients that it is a veritable superfood, sweet and fragrant with spice and shot through with bright green and gold.

ZUCCHINI BREAD
2½ c. zucchini (about 2 large), grated
½ c. whole wheat pastry flour
2 Tbsp. flaxseed meal
1 c. unbleached all-purpose flour
1 tsp. turmeric
2 tsp. Vietnamese cinnamon
Generous ½ tsp. salt
1 tsp. baking powder
½ tsp. baking soda
2 eggs, beaten
½ c. raw sugar
½ c. vegetable oil
2 tsp. vanilla extract
½ c. chopped walnuts, optional

Preheat oven to 350 degrees. Grease 2 medium loaf pans (1.5 quart), 3 small loaf pans, 2 muffin tins or 4 mini-muffin tins. Grate zucchini and set aside while making batter. Do not drain the liquid let by the zucchinis; it is part of the recipe.

In a small bowl, stir together dry ingredients except sugar and walnuts (if using). In a separate, larger bowl, whisk or beat together eggs, sugar, oil, and vanilla until thick and lemony colored, about 1 to 2 minutes. Fold shredded zucchini and any liquid it has let into egg mixture until well blended. Stir in dry ingredients, mixing just until blended. Add walnuts if desired.

Pour into prepared pans and bake for about 40 to 45 minutes for medium loaves, 30 to 40 minutes for small loaves, 15 to 20 minutes for muffins, or 12 to 15 for mini-muffins. Check that it's done: the tester should still have crumbs stuck to it, but no wet batter. Do not overbake.

Allow to cool before removing from pan. Delicious for breakfast with a smear of cream cheese, or with a savory soup like Harira. For a light dessert, try icing as below.

CINNAMON VANILLA ICING
1 c. confectioners' sugar, sifted
1 - 2 Tbsp. milk, cream, or almond milk
1 tsp. vanilla extract
¼ tsp. Vietnamese cinnamon
¼ tsp. salt

Whisk all ingredients well, until you achieve a smooth, slightly runny icing. Pour or drizzle over completely cooled zucchini bread/muffins and allow to harden for at least a half hour before serving.

PUMPKIN CHOCOLATE CHIP VARIATION
Substitute one **15-oz. can of pureed plain pumpkin** for the zucchini. Add ½ **tsp. ginger** instead of the turmeric, and stir in ¼ **c. each of bittersweet and milk chocolate chips** (or chopped chocolate bars). The baking time remains the same and this loaf really needs no icing, as it is quite rich enough with the chocolate accents. Especially delicious with a cup of hot coffee for a quiet weekend breakfast.

Makes about 24 muffins or 48 mini muffins; or 1 large or 3 mini-loaves.

BLUEBERRY GINGERBREAD

My childhood memories of gingerbread center around baked cookies with lemon peel and chocolate—a popular German holiday treat called *lebkuchen*. I was never a great fan; gingerbread looked and smelled appetizing enough, but it always tasted dry, even in cookie form.

Decades later, I was leafing through my favorite little baking book, *Quick Breads* by Beatrice A. Ojakangas, and I found an intriguing recipe for blueberry gingerbread, an unfamiliar combination. The blueberries, it turned out, added more moisture and contrast, nestled in little beds of gingery cake. I was hooked.

The recipe here is the result of my inevitable tinkering: the relatively short baking time ensures the gingerbread stays truly moist, and decreasing the sugar brings the spices to the foreground. The addition of a bit of fine whole wheat flour brings a toasty density to the bread without drying it out. I call for frozen blueberries because I think of it as a winter dish, but if you decide to bake it in blueberry season, by all means use fresh instead. Finally, I find that this recipe benefits greatly from a fresh batch of ground ginger. The flavor will be that much brighter, holding its own with the rich molasses and cinnamon, and your house will smell divine. I love this combination so much that now, I can't imagine a winter without it.

1 egg
½ c. vegetable oil
½ c. dark brown sugar
½ c. blackstrap molasses
2 c. frozen wild blueberries, or fresh
1 Tbsp. raw sugar, if needed for berries
1 ½ c. unbleached all-purpose flour
½ c. whole wheat pastry flour
1 tsp. baking soda
1 tsp. ground cinnamon
1 tsp. ground ginger
½ tsp. salt
1 c. buttermilk (or almond milk)*

Preheat oven to 350 degrees. Grease two medium (1.5-quart) loaf pans or one 9-inch square baking pan.

*If you don't have buttermilk, you can make a quick version by adding 1 tsp. lemon juice to 1 cup regular milk (or almond milk, if making nondairy), stir and let it sit for 5 minutes until slightly curdled.

In a large mixing bowl, beat egg, oil, and brown sugar until light. Add molasses and beat again until thick, like dark caramel. In a small bowl, toss the frozen blueberries with 1 Tbsp. raw sugar and 2 Tbsp. of the white flour until well coated. (If you are using fresh berries and they are pretty sweet, just skip the extra sugar here.) In a third bowl, mix the rest of the flour with the remaining dry ingredients.

Add the flour mixture alternately with the buttermilk to the molasses mixture, blending on a low setting or with a spoon until fully integrated. Fold in the blueberries.

Turn batter into prepared pan and bake for 35 to 40 minutes for loaves, about 40 to 45 minutes for square pan, until a tester in the center comes out with a moist crumb still clinging to it, but no wet batter.

Serve warm for breakfast (or elevenses!) on a cold winter morning or a bright early fall day, with a smear of cream cheese or chèvre and a cup of Earl Grey tea. Also lovely as a light dessert with fresh, slightly sweet whipped cream. *Makes about 16 to 20 squares of gingerbread.*

COOKING TIPS TO LIVE BY

MIREPOIX

Mirepoix is a French term referring to the classic mixture of onions, celery, and carrots that forms the base of a large number of soups, stews, and sauces in Western cooking, by creating a balance of sweet, aromatic, and sharp flavors. The term comes from the title of the duc de Lévis-Mirepoix, an eighteenth-century Frenchman who first identified this mixture as a staple in French cooking. Taking the time to make a flavorful, fragrant base is a key to great soups.

SWEATING AND CARAMELIZING ONIONS

Many of my savory recipes begin with onions that I instruct you to "sweat" or "caramelize." These are two different processes that can sometimes be combined. Sweating onions means sautéing them until they turn translucent and begin to bring their natural sugars to the surface. Caramelizing is a longer process that involves getting the onions to render even more of those natural sugars without burning—something sugars tend to do easily. This requires a bit of patience and experience; if you cook onions at the right temperature for long enough, you will get a glorious caramel color and a soft, sweet concoction you can use in a multitude of delectable dishes.

SOUPS

BEST CHICKEN SOUP

The Jewish people have been making chicken soup for hundreds of years. In *shtetls* and other poor communities, that chicken was often the only meat they ate all week (or sometimes all year). It was frequently served at the festive meal before the fast of Yom Kippur, the Day of Atonement that follows the Jewish new year. (Leave it to us to start the year off with apologies, right?) The Eastern European tradition was to serve the rich broth with some kind of dumplings—either matzah balls or *kreplach* (dumplings filled with potatoes or meat). This made it more filling so it stretched that much further. Nowadays, the base of Ashkenazi chicken soup is most often a mixture of onions, celery, and carrots—what the French call *mirepoix*. (See Cooking Tips to Live By for more.) In centuries past, chicken soup has also included any number of other root vegetables, like parsnips, which continue to be a popular addition in some circles.

Whatever vegetables it contains, it is no lie that chicken soup will cure what ails you. Research shows that when it is prepared from scratch, it has anti-inflammatory effects due to an amino acid released in the chicken fat, called cysteine, which is said to help with bronchitis and asthma. Of course, the hot liquid and the steam can't hurt, either. Comfort food does have a way of, well, giving comfort.

Preparation of this soup is time-consuming, so I don't recommend trying to make it if you're the one who's sick. But it is one heck of a soup, and well worth your time if you are making it for someone in need, you want to bring joy to those at your daily table, or you just want to knock your friends' socks off.

Total preparation and cooking time: 2½ hours. You will need a sheet of cheesecloth to make this soup.

2 - 3 Tbsp. extra virgin olive oil (or rendered chicken fat, schmaltz)
2 large sweet onions (like Mayan or Vidalia)
1 bunch celery, chopped, including greens
1 lb. carrots, sliced
Salt and pepper to taste
3 - 4 quarts chicken broth
1 whole pullet or cut-up fryer chicken

Preheat a large stockpot on medium-high, adding olive oil or schmaltz when hot, and allowing it to liquefy for a moment. (See Kasha Varnishkes for instructions on how to render chicken fat.)

Dice onions large and add to pot. Once you've got a good sizzle, turn temperature down to medium to prevent burning or too much browning. Stir occasionally until the onions start to sweat (turn translucent and let out moisture), usually about 15 minutes. Add the celery and stir to coat, sautéing again until they begin to soften as well, another 5 to 10 minutes. Add carrots and just enough broth to cover the veggies. Bring to a boil, add 1 tsp. salt and several grinds of black pepper, and cook for about 30 to 40 minutes until the *mirepoix* is completely soft.

If you want to make a vegetarian soup base as well, which I do on a regular basis for any vegetarians in my orbit, use vegetable broth (or bouillon with water) as your starting liquid. Once you've cooked the veggies down, separate them into two batches; extra *mirepoix* is a good idea if making two versions of the soup.

Rinse chicken and tie up in a large sheet of cheesecloth (make a bundle: four corners toward the middle, tied in two double knots). Place cheesecloth-wrapped chicken on top of the soft-cooked *mirepoix* and add enough liquid to just lift the bundle. Bring to a boil, then turn down and simmer, covered, for 90 minutes; make sure to set a timer. When time is up, place a bowl next to the stove. Carefully lift chicken bundle from pot with a long-handled spoon or tongs and place in the bowl to drain. Be sure to save all of the liquid that drips out to put back in the pot. When cool enough to handle, cut or untie the bundle and let chicken cool further, until you can pull all the meat and skin off the bones. Return meat and drippings to the pot. Discard skin and bones. Gently rewarm the soup, adding salt and pepper as needed. Do not boil.

Serve with matzah balls, egg noodles, or rice, but **do not** put any of these starches directly into the soup. They will turn to glop. I only had to make this mistake once—at a dinner party—to remember it for the rest of my life. Cook and keep the starch separate, and serve directly into bowls with the hot soup on top.

When cold, the chicken fat in the soup will separate, but do not skim it off or the flavor and nutritional value will be compromised. The fat will melt and reintegrate with the soup when it is warmed up. Keeps in fridge for several days, and freezes well. *Makes about 10 to 12 servings.*

If you made it through this whole process, I hope you will sit down and enjoy the soup with your loved ones. Take a breath, inhale the wonderful fragrance, and let it nourish you all the way down to your toes.

TOMATO BISQUE

Contrary to popular opinion, tomatoes did not originate in Italy, but in the Americas; they grew as wild plants for a couple of thousand years, especially around the Andes Mountains, before they were introduced to Europe in the sixteenth century. The tomato has since become one of the most beloved fruits in the world—it is technically a fruit, since it grows from a flower and has seeds—and though Italy has certainly made the most of it, the tomato is used for countless savory dishes in every part of the globe.

While it is true that traditional bisques are made with seafood stock, what distinguishes them from other soups in my mind is their thickness and their use of cream—or in this case, cream cheese. I first found a variation of this creamed tomato soup in the *California Kosher* cookbook, and it reminded me instantly of the Swiss tomato soup from my childhood that I had been trying to replicate for years. I played with the recipe until I got it as close as possible to the flavor and texture I remembered, using fresh basil and fresh tomatoes, increasing the salt, garlic, and onions, and blending the soup to a smooth, creamy finish after it's cooked. Neufchatel is a soft, unripened French cheese very similar to American cream cheese—either one will work perfectly to add a silky richness and turn the soup a gorgeous sunrise shade of pinkish orange.

When summer tomatoes and basil are at their peak, this tomato bisque is an explosion of flavor. It's best eaten in small quantities and at room temperature. Try it with some crusty bread—or better yet, a classic grilled cheese—and a small salad of greens. Though the ingredients are simple, I think it's pretty special.

2 large sweet onions, roughly chopped
2 Tbsp. extra virgin olive oil
2 Tbsp. butter
1 tsp. salt, or more to taste
Large handful fresh basil leaves
3 cloves garlic, minced
3 large, ripe tomatoes, chopped
1 28-oz. can crushed tomatoes
1 tomato can of water
Freshly ground black pepper to taste
¼ c. dry sherry or white wine (optional)
2 Tbsp. honey or agave
8 oz. Neufchatel or cream cheese

Roughly chop the onions. Melt the butter and 1 Tbsp. olive oil in a heavy-bottomed soup pot on medium heat. Add onions to pot with ¼ tsp. salt, cooking on medium until they become translucent. Continue cooking until onions soften and begin to render their sugars, about 15 minutes, turning down heat to medium low so they do not caramelize all the way to brownness.

Chiffonade basil by stacking the leaves and rolling into a cylinder. Cut crosswise with a sharp knife to make thin ribbons. This bruises basil less than rough chopping, and it will look so pretty among the tomatoes.

Add remainder of olive oil, turn up heat, and add garlic, chopped fresh tomatoes, and chiffonaded basil leaves. Cook until tomatoes begin to break down and become paler in color, about 10 to 15 minutes. Add the crushed tomatoes, refill empty can with water and add to pot along with salt and pepper. Simmer for 20 to 30 minutes on medium until flavors begin to come together, stirring occasionally.

Just before removing from heat, stir in sherry or white wine if desired. Remove from heat and add honey or agave; adjust salt and pepper. Drop in cream cheese or Neufchatel by spoonfuls, stirring until they dissolve. Using a handheld or immersion blender on medium, blend in bursts of one minute at a time, being careful not to splash yourself. If using a regular blender, I recommend you wait until liquid cools somewhat. Blend until the soup is smooth and creamy. Delicious served warm, room temperature, or cold on a hot summer's day. *Makes about 8 to 10 servings.*

MINESTRONE WITH SHELLS AND MOZZARELLA

I think of minestrone as the king of soups: it is nutritious, beautiful, and filling, and it pretty much makes a meal on its own. Though it is a perennial favorite, Italians don't view it as a royal dish; in fact, they consider it part of the cooking tradition known as *la cucina povera* or "cooking of the poor"—in other words, peasant food. The dishes that fit into this tradition are the ones that involve throwing together whatever is at hand. In the Italian countryside, this could mean grabbing a crust of stale bread, some tomatoes and onions, basil from the garden, a glug of olive oil or balsamico, and suddenly, you have *panzanella* (bread salad). Minestrone has been in existence for millennia. It has gone through an endless number of iterations, the most recent of which is the wonderfully familiar tomato-based broth thickened with beans and often pasta, flavored with garlic and basil, and host to a wide variety of vegetables.

My first encounter with minestrone was at *il pranza di domenica*—otherwise known as Sunday lunch, Italian style—in Donoratico, the small town in the Livorno region of Italy where my family used to vacation. From where we lived in Zurich we could simply get in the car, drive over the San Bernardino pass, and be there within a few hours. These trips, beginning when I was about four, also began my lifelong love affair with the ocean. During that particular trip, my parents befriended a fisherman named Bruno whose family lived near the beach cabin we were renting, and one Sunday he invited us to share in his large family's midday meal. And what a meal it was: It went on for three hours, starting with a soup course (minestrone!) followed by a pasta course with lasagna and homemade long pasta, and then an enormous fish course with boundless varieties of seafood, and then dessert. There were long pauses between courses, but still, the size of that dinner broke the bounds of my wildest imagination; I'm not sure, to this day, that any other feast has come close. The sensations of the meal, the vibrant, sun-drenched colors, the steam, the warm smell of garlic, the beautiful music of the Italian language—I will never forget it.

This is my humble attempt to recreate the memory of that first minestrone. It is not a quick soup: it takes a good hour to make, and incidentally, tastes better the second day, so if you can bring yourself to wait overnight, the flavors will deepen considerably. When you're ready, if you choose to serve it as I usually do, ladled over a bed of pasta shells and topped with grated mozzarella cheese, you can bet that everyone will leave the table too full for one more bite. That is, unless you make dessert. Torta Caprese, anyone?

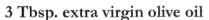

3 Tbsp. extra virgin olive oil
2 large onions, chopped
1 lb. cremini or white mushrooms, sliced
4 cloves garlic, minced
1 Tbsp. salt, or more to taste
3 Tbsp. tomato paste
1 large bunch basil, chiffonaded
1 lb. zucchini, diced
2 28-oz. cans crushed Italian tomatoes
2 tomato cans water
2 Tbsp. honey
1 Tbsp. dried oregano
1 Tbsp. dried basil
Freshly ground black pepper to taste
2 cans small red or kidney beans
1 c. red wine, or more to taste
2 - 4 c. additional water as needed
½ lb. green beans or haricots verts
½ lb. baby spinach
1 lb. shells, cooked al dente, tossed with a little oil
8 oz. mozzarella, grated, for serving

In a large, preheated soup pot, place 2 Tbsp. olive oil and allow a minute for it to liquefy. Add chopped onions, turn heat down to medium, and sweat onions until they become translucent and begin to render their sugars, about 10 to 15 minutes. I don't use a typical *mirepoix* (classic soup base of onion-celery-carrots) in this soup because there are so many other wonderful flavors—but it certainly wouldn't be out of place. (For more about *mirepoix*, see Cooking Tips to Live By.)

While onions are cooking, wipe mushrooms with a damp cloth and slice thick. Add to pot along with minced garlic, 1 tsp. salt, and tomato paste, whisking to combine with the liquid in the pot. Turn heat up a bit and cook until the garlic is very fragrant and mushrooms have let their liquid, about 5 to 7 minutes.

To chiffonade basil, stack leaves and roll into a cylinder, cutting crosswise to make thin ribbons. Add diced zucchini, half of basil, and another Tbsp. olive oil to the pot, and sauté for several more minutes. When zucchini is bright green, add canned tomatoes. Fill both cans with water and add as well. Add dried basil, oregano, remainder of salt, honey, and several good grinds of black pepper. Turn heat up to high and bring soup to a boil. Drain and rinse canned beans, and add once soup is boiling, along with red wine and 2 to 4 cups water (depending how thick you want your soup). Return soup to a boil, then turn down to simmer. Cook for about 45 minutes, stirring occasionally, and checking that beans are not sticking or burning. (You will add spinach, green beans, and remainder of basil at the end of that time.)

While soup is simmering, cook pasta shells until just al dente, drain and rinse, then toss with a bit of olive oil so they don't stick together. Place in a bowl and cover. I do not add them to the soup, though that might be more traditional—I prefer to keep them separate so they don't get too soft or absorb a lot of the tomato broth. Grate mozzarella into a second bowl, cover, and set both pasta and cheese aside until minestrone is ready to serve.

Now back to the soup: Add remainder of fresh basil and whole bag of spinach, and turn heat up a bit so soup continues to bubble. The spinach will look enormous going in, but it will wilt down into the soup within a few minutes. Trim green beans and cut into 2-inch pieces, add to pot, and simmer for ten more minutes. Turn off soup and allow to rest while you set the table. Or cool and place in the fridge to serve the next day; reheat on medium low for about half an hour. If you are doing it this way, you can wait to grate the cheese and cook the pasta until the next day, or do it now and reheat pasta just before serving. Then you will have the satisfaction of knowing that there is nothing you need to do for dinner tomorrow.

Serve in large, deep bowls, with pasta placed in first, then hot soup, then grated mozzarella on top. It will melt gorgeously into the soup, and come out again on your spoon in creamy strands. Be sure to have plenty of napkins on hand. *Makes about 8 to 12 servings.*

HARIRA (LAMB AND LENTIL SOUP)

Harira is a traditional Moroccan dish, often used to break the fast after Yom Kippur or, in the Islamic community, during Ramadan. This recipe, with the addition of lemon juice, is a signature of Sephardic Jewish cuisine. The Sephardi Jews flourished in Spain and Portugal until their expulsion during the Spanish Inquisition, when they were scattered across the globe. After hundreds of years in the diaspora, their rich cultural traditions still live on in dishes like this one.

Some of the flavors in this soup (cinnamon and lemon juice) might be unexpected in this setting, but they come together in the most marvelous way. This recipe doubles well, and is sure to please with its contrast of rich lamb, hearty lentils, sweet, fragrant cinnamon, and the zing of fresh lemon juice.

2 Tbsp. olive oil
1 large onion, chopped
3 stalks celery with greens, thinly chopped
¼ c. chopped fresh parsley
1 tsp. turmeric
1 tsp. cinnamon
1 lb. lamb shoulder, trimmed
½ c. dried lentils, washed and drained
6 c. chicken stock
2 Tbsp. tomato paste
1 tsp. salt or more, plus freshly ground black pepper to taste
2 - 4 Tbsp. fresh lemon juice

Preheat olive oil in a soup pot and add chopped onions. Sauté on medium-high until onions are translucent, about 10 minutes. Add celery, parsley, turmeric, and cinnamon, and continue cooking on medium, stirring often, until celery begins to soften and becomes fragrant, another 10 minutes. Trim fat from lamb and cut into 2-inch cubes, adding to pot and turning often until meat is lightly browned, about 15 minutes. Add lentils, chicken stock, and tomato paste, stirring until paste is integrated. Bring soup just to a boil, then lower to a strong simmer and cook until lentils are soft, about 45 minutes. Add salt and pepper to taste. Just before serving, add lemon juice, stirring well to achieve a marked lemon flavor. *Serves about 6 to 8.*

NEW ENGLAND CORN CHOWDER

Chowders and New England go together like…music and dance. Right? That's certainly become the case, but it is likely the French who first brought this traditional dish of Breton fishermen to the area. In fact, the word "chowder" appears to be derived from the French *chaudière*, meaning "cauldron." The most popular New England variety is clam chowder, perhaps due to the abundance of these small, sweet shellfish in northern Atlantic waters. My father adored clam chowder, and I remember it fondly from my years growing up along the Connecticut shoreline.

When I was keeping a kosher home, clams (and all forms of shellfish) were out of bounds; I tried my hand at a number of other fish chowders, but it was always the one made with just vegetables that I found the most satisfying: sweet summer corn, tender chunks of golden potatoes, aromatic celery, and bright, sweet rounds of carrots.

This soup is best made in the summer, when corn is at its peak. If you can get hold of some Vidalia or Mayan sweet onions, all the better. The sweet with the savory is the name of the game here. If you're making it in the winter—which I have done many times as well, if only to be reminded of summer's warmth—you will need to use frozen corn which is not as sweet, so you might want to add a couple of tablespoons of agave or honey to the pot. You also might need to season it a bit more heavily to achieve the desired intensity of flavor. Either way, this is a thick and satisfying soup that is really a meal in itself.

If you want to make this dish vegan, substitute additional olive oil for the butter, and try coconut milk and/ or coconut cream instead of dairy milk and cream. Or substitute one cup of an unsweetened nondairy alternative and set aside one-fourth of the soup veggies in their liquid to cream in a blender, adding it back into the pot afterward. This will make the soup creamier without adding fat.

Tarragon is an herb that has a slightly sweet, almost-licorice flavor; some people love it (I among them) and others, not so much. I think it makes a natural dancing partner for corn, but if you are not a fan, thyme and sage are other lovely herbs to pair with corn. And if you decide to try making it with coconut milk instead of cream, cilantro is a natural partner to coconut, and would make a perfect garnish for the chowder. No matter how you make it, this sunny, sweet chowder is always a favorite.

4 c. vegetable broth or water
4 - 5 ears of corn, or 3 c. frozen
2 Tbsp. extra virgin olive oil
2 Tbsp. butter
2 large sweet onions, chopped
One bunch celery, chopped
4 - 6 carrots, peeled
4 yellow potatoes, peeled
1 Tbsp. salt, or more to taste
Freshly ground black pepper to taste
1 bunch fresh tarragon (or 1 tsp. dried)
1 tsp. smoked paprika, optional
2 c. whole milk
½ c. heavy cream

Bring the water or broth to boil in a large pot. Shuck corn and boil for five minutes. Remove corn with tongs and allow to cool, leaving the water/broth in the pot. Cut the bottoms off the cobs so they will stand flat on their ends; remove kernels by using a clean downward motion with a sharp knife. Set the kernels aside, and place the naked cobs back into the liquid to continue simmering—this creates a corn stock that will intensify the flavor of the soup when you combine it with the vegetables later.

In a second soup pot, preheat olive oil and butter, add chopped onions and sauté on medium high until softened and turning translucent. Add chopped carrots and celery with their green tops, and sauté until the *mirepoix* is brightly colored. Peel and cut potatoes into large cubes, adding to soup pot. Ladle in enough corn stock from first pot just to cover vegetables, and add the salt. Bring to a boil, turn down to simmer, and cook until all veggies are soft, 30 to 40 minutes.

Roughly chop tarragon and add along with paprika, if using. Place a strainer over soup pot and carefully pour remainder of corn stock through, catching cobs and silks (to discard). Add corn kernels and simmer just to heat through. Turn down to low, add milk and cream, stir to combine. Taste and adjust seasonings.

This chowder is truly wonderful with warm, buttered Honey Cornbread and an All-Green Salad, or with a slice of Famous Squash Pie on the side. *Serves about 6 to 8.*

POPPI'S MUSHROOM BARLEY SOUP

This soup is an old family favorite, and especially good in winter. Barley is an ancient grain—one of the earliest to have been domesticated, and one of the most enduring, due to its short growing time. When it's cooked in liquid, barley becomes creamy, a bit like oatmeal, and expands greatly in size. It has a slightly nutty flavor, but its relative neutrality means it absorbs the stronger flavors of the foods it is paired with. Mushrooms, with their robust, almost beefy flavor, make a perfect partner for barley.

Eating this soup invariably reminds me of my father, Myron, who died just about a year ago as I am writing this. My sweet grandson, Asher, came into the world only six weeks later, and inherited my father's Hebrew name, Meir, as his middle name. My Poppi was a very particular eater (no cheese, vinegar, and barely any fruits or vegetables. As you can imagine, my mom had quite a time cooking for him!) But he loved mushrooms and onions, and for many years before he died, he ate mushroom barley soup just about every day for lunch. Sometimes he would have it with a piece of toast, or some matzah with whipped butter—he and my mother were the only people I knew who ate matzah all year round. But he loved this soup every time, and I must say that on an icy day, there is nothing more warming than a bowl of it. The mushrooms impart a dark, meaty flavor, and the barley makes it creamy, nutritious, and filling.

2 - 3 Tbsp. extra virgin olive oil
2 large onions, chopped (I like Mayan Sweets or Vidalias, which don't make you cry unless you are thinking about how much your father would have loved this soup)
2 lb. cremini (Baby Bella) mushrooms, sliced
6 carrots, sliced
1 whole bunch celery
1 - 2 tsp. salt, or more to taste
8 - 12 c. beef or vegetable broth
1½ c. pearled barley
¼ c. dry sherry or white wine, optional
Freshly ground black pepper to taste

Note: Don't use more barley than the recipe calls for; it grows exponentially in the soup as it cooks.

Place oil in bottom of a preheated soup pot and allow a moment for it to liquefy. Turn flame to medium-high, add chopped onions, and stir occasionally as they begin to brown, about 15 minutes.

Wipe mushrooms with a damp cloth and slice. Add to pot and sauté until they begin to let their liquid. (Because of the mushrooms, this soup's *mirepoix*—classic onion-celery-carrot mixture—is not made in the usual order. For more about *mirepoix*, see Cooking Tips to Live By.) Chop carrots and celery including leaves, and add to pot with 1 tsp. salt and enough broth to cover. Continue cooking until vegetables are soft and have generated a nice brown stock. Add remaining broth, another tsp. salt, and barley. Bring to a boil, then turn down to a simmer (still bubbling, but gently).

Allow to simmer for 45 to 60 minutes, checking from time to time that barley isn't sticking, until it is soft and has doubled in size. When barley is done, add sherry or wine, if adding. Cook for 10 more minutes and adjust seasonings. Don't stint on the salt, as barley tends to absorb all the flavor you can throw at it.

This soup, like most, is even better the second day. It will thicken overnight in the fridge, so you might need to thin it with a bit more broth or water. Warm gently so barley doesn't stick, and taste to adjust salt levels before serving again. Serve with a crusty baguette—or a crispy piece of matzah and butter—for lunch. *Makes about 10 to 12 servings.*

ZUCCHINI VICHYSSOISE

This dish is a variation on vichyssoise, the cold potato-leek soup that is considered a classic of French cuisine. The addition of zucchini, a member of the gourd family native to Central America and Mexico, confirms its place on our family's list of favorite Euro-American hybrids. In reality, this is not the first Atlantic crossing for vichyssoise, but at least its third: the French began making potato-leek soup after the Spanish colonized Peru in the sixteenth century and carried the wondrous potato back to Europe with them. And the legendary cold version, as it turns out, was introduced at the New York Ritz Carlton in 1917 by French chef Louis Diat. Recalling the childhood pleasure of adding cold milk to his mother's potato soup on hot summer days, he began serving it that way in his restaurant. It became a sensation, and was enshrined in the culinary canon by Julia Child in her own classic, *Mastering the Art of French Cooking*.

When I was growing up, we returned to Switzerland every couple of summers so my father could meet with his employers at the *Neue Zürcher Zeitung* where he worked as an editor and translator, and we could all reconnect with our old friends. I tasted vichyssoise for the first time on one of these trips, when we took a drive into France for a few days. I was a teenager, feverish with existential angst, and the soup's soothing chill seemed to go straight into my veins. Decades later, I found myself returning to that memory one summer when I had a house full of agitated, hungry, teenagers of my own. It was too hot for warm soup, and the zucchinis were everywhere, demanding to be used. Before I knew it, I had this lovely green vichyssoise, lighter than its French cousin, but deeply satisfying and so beautiful! In this recipe, the buttery golden potatoes, rich cream, and delicate leeks are pumped up with sweet summer onions, bright zucchinis, and the distinctive zing of white pepper, making cool waves of endless flavor that might just become an all-time summer favorite for your family, too.

2 Tbsp. butter
2 Tbsp. extra virgin olive oil
2 large sweet onions, chopped
4 leeks, washed well and chopped (or 1 extra onion)
4 large zucchinis, cut into large rounds
6 potatoes, pref. Yukon Gold, peeled and cut into chunks
4 c. vegetable broth or chicken stock
2 tsp. sea salt or more to taste
¼ to ½ tsp. white pepper, to taste
1 c. heavy cream (or 1½ c. unsweetened nondairy substitute)

Place butter and half of olive oil in preheated soup pot, allowing to liquefy briefly. (Soup can be made nondairy by replacing the butter with more olive oil and using 1½ c. soy or other unsweetened nondairy substitute in place of cream.) Add chopped onions and leeks (if using), sautéing on medium-high until onions are translucent and leeks are bright green. Turn heat to medium low and cook for another 15 minutes, letting onions render their sugars and leeks soften. Add chopped zucchini and remainder of oil, sautéing until zucchini turns bright green. Add peeled potato chunks, vegetable broth, and half the salt.

Bring mixture to a boil. Turn down to a simmer, letting the vegetables slip beneath the surface of the broth. Continue simmering on medium low for 45 to 60 minutes, until all vegetables are completely soft and beginning to disintegrate. Stir occasionally to be sure potatoes are not sticking.

Turn off heat and use a handheld or immersion blender to cream the soup, being careful not to splash yourself. (If you don't have one, a regular blender will do, but I recommend letting the soup cool considerably before you try to ladle it out.) When all the lumps are gone and the soup is creamy and smooth, add the white pepper and remainder of salt to taste, then pour in the cream and blend once more.

Delicious served cold on a blistering summer's day, but taste and adjust salt and white pepper just before serving, as it is harder to taste seasonings in cold dishes. Also wonderful served warm in cooler weather, alongside a crusty, fresh baguette with butter and slices of sharp cheddar. *Makes about 8 to 10 servings.*

SUMMER-WINTER SOUP

This is a surprising and very pretty soup, inspired by Susie Fishbein's "Winter White" soup in *Kosher by Design Entertains*. Fishbein's innovative recipes taught me a great deal as a young cook with a kosher kitchen about how to be creative—even within the confines of those biblical laws. I have made her recipe my own with several changes, but I always want to give credit where it's due. I have changed the balance of some of her ingredients here, adding cauliflower, and substituting sweet onions for the harder-to-find leeks. I have based my pesto recipe on one given to me by my dear friend, Miranda, whose suggestion of using walnuts creates a slightly stronger flavor than the more common pine nuts.

I discovered the joys of creaming cauliflower relatively recently, and it was a revelation (see also Creamed Cauliflower). It makes an ideal base for this soup. I hope you play with the recipe and add any winter veggies you want, as long as the blended result is creamy white and smooth. The contrast of the white soup with the final flourish of pesto makes for a beautiful presentation. If you can't get hold of fresh basil, you might have to get creative with the pesto. (In years when I am thinking ahead, I remember to put pesto in the freezer during summer for such occasions.) You might even resort to a jar of prepared pesto—just try to make sure the ingredients are very similar to the ones in this recipe. Follow your bliss, but don't make yourself crazy. For me, that's what cooking is all about—along with those beguiling contrasts: white and green, summer and winter, sharp and sweet.

SOUP
2 Tbsp. extra virgin olive oil
2 sweet onions, diced
3 parsnips, peeled and cut
1 whole cauliflower, roughly chopped
4 large white potatoes, peeled and diced
2 - 3 c. chicken or vegetable stock
About 2 c. whole milk (or nondairy substitute)
1 tsp. salt or more, and freshly ground black pepper to taste

Preheat a large pot and add oil, allowing it to liquefy. Add the onions and let them sweat, turning down heat enough to soften them without browning.

Add remaining veggies, stir to coat with oil, then add 1 tsp. salt and several grinds black pepper, plus enough stock to cover. Bring to a boil, turn down, and simmer vegetables until very soft—30 to 45 minutes. Make pesto while soup is cooking (see below).

When vegetables are completely broken down, use an immersion blender to cream them, being careful not to splash yourself. Add enough milk (or substitutes) for a thick and creamy consistency, and adjust seasonings to taste, whirring once more with blender.

PESTO
4 cloves chopped garlic
40 or 50 fresh basil leaves
½ c. walnuts
1½ c. Parmesan, pref. Parmigiano Reggiano
½ c. extra virgin olive oil
¼ tsp. sea salt, or more to taste
Freshly ground black pepper

Blend garlic and basil in food processor, stopping to scrape sides once or twice with a rubber spatula. Add walnuts, and blend again; add cheese and repeat, scraping sides of bowl each time to loosen stubborn bits. For more about Parmigiano Reggiano, see Serena's "Noonies." (This pesto can be made vegan by omitting Parmesan and adding a bit more salt to the mixture. It will, of course, taste different, but it will still be delicious.) With the food processor running, add extra virgin olive oil in a slow stream. Keep blending until mixture is bright green, oil is incorporated, and it looks creamy and integrated. Add salt and pepper to taste. Set aside until ready to serve, covering pesto with a thin layer of olive oil to keep it bright green.

To serve Summer-Winter Soup, ladle hot soup into bowls at the table, adding a dollop of pesto to each bowl and giving a small, slow stir to achieve a pretty green swirl in the center of the white soup. Guests can stir it in completely or dip into the swirl of pesto as they wish. This presentation is so lovely and allows everyone to get as much pesto as they want in each spoonful; if there is extra pesto, pass it around.

If not serving immediately, warm soup gently, and let pesto come to room temperature at the same time. This is a wonderful first course, but serve small portions—it's surprisingly filling. *Serves about 8 to 12.*

ITALIAN WEDDING SOUP

I started writing this cookbook in honor of my daughter Gabriella's wedding—now over seven years ago—so this recipe was always destined to be included. In Italy, where this soup originated, it is called *minestra marita*: "married soup" or "husband soup." Though it is certainly good enough to serve at a wedding, this dish actually got its name because of the marriage of meat and greens at its center.

A certain point comes every winter when I just have to make this soup. I crave the meatballs and greens, the fragrant broth poured over pasta and swimming with garlic. I usually make my meatballs with grass-fed ground beef, but bison and ground turkey work nicely, too. (I don't recommend all-white meat ground turkey, as it's too lean to make a juicy meatball.) The addition of rolled oats to the ground meat, eggs, and spices is my substitute for the bread found in most Italian meatballs; I think it tastes lighter. I wouldn't go so far as to say that this soup is as good as any husband, but it can sure keep you warm on a cold night.

<u>SOUP</u>
2 Tbsp. extra virgin olive oil
2 sweet onions, chopped
3 cloves minced garlic
4 carrots, chopped
8 celery ribs, chopped
1 tsp salt, or more to taste
Freshly ground black pepper to taste
2 Tbsp. fresh tarragon (or 1 tsp. dried)
1 tsp. dried parsley
12 c. chicken stock or broth
4 bay leaves
18 oz. washed baby spinach
1 lb. short pasta (like shells or orecchiette), al dente

In a large soup pot, preheat 2 Tbsp. olive oil. Add onions and cook on medium high until they soften. Add minced garlic and continue cooking until onions begin to caramelize, about 15 minutes. Add celery, carrots, tarragon, and parsley, and cook until soft, adding a little chicken broth or more oil if sticking.

MEATBALLS

2 lbs. lean ground beef (or bison or dark meat turkey), pref. grass-fed
2 eggs
¼ c. rolled oats (not instant)
2 Tbsp. dried minced onion
2 cloves minced garlic
1 Tbsp. fresh tarragon (or 1 tsp. dried)
1 tsp. dried parsley
¼ to ½ tsp. salt
Freshly ground black pepper
¼ to ½ c. chicken broth
2 Tbsp. extra virgin olive oil

While soup vegetables cook, set a pot of salted water to boil for pasta, then begin making meatballs.

In a medium bowl, combine meat, eggs, rolled oats, dried minced onion, garlic, herbs, and salt and pepper. Mix until well combined. Roll tablespoons of mixture between hands to form into meatballs. I like making my meatballs small so there are more of them; if you prefer them larger, just adjust your cooking time to make sure they are done all the way through before you add them to the soup pot.

Preheat a large skillet and add 2 Tbsp. olive oil. Drop meatballs in skillet and sauté in 2 or 3 batches until cooked through and lightly browned all over, about 8 to 15 minutes a batch, depending on size. Add 1 to 2 Tbsp. chicken broth at a time to each batch to prevent meatballs from sticking or burning. When all meatballs are browned, keep them warm in the skillet along with their drippings.

Now is a good time to make the pasta. Cook al dente, rinse, and set aside for serving. Do not put in soup.

Turn back to the soup pot. Add bay leaves and remainder of chicken broth to veggies and bring to a boil, then turn down to a simmer. Drop cooked meatballs into soup. Pour a ladle of soup into the still-hot meatball skillet to loosen all the drippings and browned bits (this is called *deglazing*). Add spinach to skillet and sauté for two or three minutes until wilted. Carefully pour contents of skillet into soup pot, and remove bay leaves from soup with a strainer or spoon. Add salt and pepper to taste, adjusting seasonings as necessary. Serve in large bowls, ladled over al dente pasta. *Makes about 10 to 12 servings. Buon appetito!*

LOUIS'S NEW FATHER SOUP (BABY KALE, WHITE BEAN, POTATO, AND VEGGIE SAUSAGE)

This soup came into the world just two days after my grandson, Asher. I asked his new dad, Louis: "Any special requests for Shabbat dinner?" Louis is a vegetarian, which makes it easier for him to keep kosher, but sometimes makes it harder for me to think of what to cook for him. He and my daughter, Gabriella, were still in the hospital with their newborn son, whose name I would not learn until a week later at his bris. The Jewish custom of withholding the name of a baby boy until it is publicly announced during this ritual is equally infuriating and enchanting. It is hard to be patient through that long week, but this custom reminds us that there is power and magic in names and they should not be given lightly.

Asher was named after Louis's father, who died suddenly when Louis was still in college. By the time Louis became a father himself, he had also become a rabbi, and was committed to observing Jewish law, which meant cooking the Sabbath meal before sundown on Friday. On that day, with the approach of Asher's first Shabbat and no rest in sight, Louis was craving comfort, and to answer my question about his requests, he reeled off a short list of his favorite foods in a sleep-deprived daze: potatoes, greens, white beans, veggie sausage. Since my options for schlepping food to the hospital were pretty limited, the only thing to do was put them all together in a pot and see what happened. The result was a garlicky, hearty winter soup with echoes of Tuscany; it tasted just as good in disposable bowls in the pediatric ward of Newton-Wellesley Hospital, as it did when they sat down at their own table for their homecoming meal.

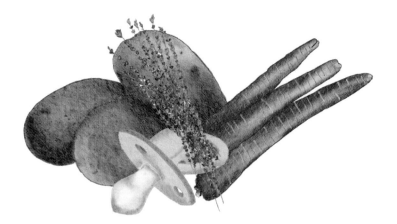

4 Tbsp. extra virgin olive oil, divided
2 large onions, chopped
1 lb. carrots, chopped
6 cloves garlic, minced
8 - 10 c. vegetable broth
1 Tbsp. dried oregano
1 Tbsp. thyme
4 large or 6 medium yellow potatoes, peeled
2 15-oz. cans small white beans
1 15-oz. can black-eyed peas
10 ounces baby kale, baby spinach, or a mixture
6 vegetarian sausage patties
Salt and fresh black pepper to taste

Heat 2 Tbsp. olive oil in a soup pot. When oil is shimmering, drop chopped onions in and turn heat to medium-high, sweating them for 15 minutes or so, until they turn translucent and begin to caramelize. Turn heat down to medium, add carrots and garlic, and stir to coat with oil, adding a bit of veggie broth to soften them as they cook. When carrots begin to soften, stir in half of the herbs and cook until fragrant.

Peel potatoes and cut into cubes, adding them to pot with enough additional broth to cover. Bring to a boil, then turn down to simmer until potatoes become soft, about 20 minutes. Drain and rinse beans and black-eyed peas. Add to the pot with remainder of broth, herbs, salt, and fresh black pepper, bringing to a boil. Add the spinach and/or kale (it will look enormous but will reduce quickly once it has wilted), stir, and turn soup down to a simmer again. Cover and allow to simmer for 30 more minutes or until all veggies are soft, leafy greens are thoroughly wilted, and it looks like soup.

While soup is simmering, place frozen veggie sausages in microwave for two minutes to defrost. Cut into one-inch pieces. Heat a large skillet with remaining 2 Tbsp. olive oil and add veggie sausage pieces, frying until crisp and brown on the outside. Add to soup, and adjust salt and pepper as needed.

Serve with a warm challah or a crusty loaf of multigrain bread and fresh butter. *Makes about 8 to 10 servings.*

COOKING TIPS TO LIVE BY

A GOOD KNIFE

A sharp, well-balanced knife is by far the most important tool you will need for your cooking adventures. The four or five dull cutting knives that most of us have in our drawers are an impediment to prep work and hard on elbows and wrists (and though it may seem counter-intuitive, they hurt much more than sharp knives if they cut you). You will want to try a few chef's knives out in a kitchen store to find one that feels good in your hand. Then keep it sharp! I sharpen my Global chef's knife weekly, so it cuts through potatoes like butter. A single, high-quality chef's knife, a small paring knife, and a simple manual sharpener are really all it takes to make prepping fruits, vegetables, and proteins faster, safer, and a lot more fun.

SALADS

ALL-GREEN SALAD WITH CLASSIC FRENCH VINAIGRETTE

The original French dressing is a classic vinaigrette, simple and savory with oil and vinegar, and maybe a bit of mustard. What Americans have come to call "French Dressing" is something else altogether—a sweet, orange dressing made from adding sugar and ketchup to a regular vinaigrette. Bottled salad dressings often contain a lot of sugar, preservatives, and thickeners, which gives them a gloppy consistency that tends to overshadow whatever lovely greens they are applied to. So try making your own; all it takes is a little lemon or red wine vinegar, an equal amount of extra virgin olive oil, and some spices. You might never look back.

SALAD
1 head green leaf lettuce, washed and torn (or baby field greens)
1 European cucumber or 2 Persian cucumbers, thinly sliced
1 perfectly ripe avocado, diced
2 - 3 Tbsp. roasted, salted pumpkin seeds (pepitas)

Combine all ingredients. When ready to serve, toss with French vinaigrette.

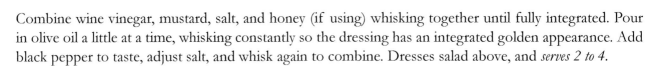

FRENCH VINAIGRETTE
3 Tbsp. red wine vinegar
1 tsp. coarse grain mustard
¼ tsp. salt and ground black pepper to taste
1 tsp. honey, optional
¼ c. extra virgin olive oil

Combine wine vinegar, mustard, salt, and honey (if using) whisking together until fully integrated. Pour in olive oil a little at a time, whisking constantly so the dressing has an integrated golden appearance. Add black pepper to taste, adjust salt, and whisk again to combine. Dresses salad above, and *serves 2 to 4.*

This is a simple salad with creamy, crunchy, and tangy notes. It pairs well with a rich dish like Summer Corn Tart, Rib Eye Steak Chimichurri, or Chicken with Roasted Garlic, Potatoes, Lemon, and Tomatoes.

FLORENTINE SHAVED FENNEL AND CABBAGE SALAD

I first encountered this salad in 2016 on my most recent trip to Italy. I was in a tiny family restaurant in Florence with my friend Jeremy and an American ex-pat, who urged us to order this salad as a starter. It was the simplest thing in the world: thinly-shaved fennel and cabbage laid side by side on a plate, drizzled with local olive oil and balsamic vinegar, and finished off with salt and fresh black pepper. That was it! But the combination of flavors was so fresh and marvelous, I could never forget it.

Fennel is a Mediterranean vegetable that grows in the shape of a layered bulb; it tastes faintly of licorice and heavily of springtime. When it is roasted, it transforms into something hearty and almost wintery (see Butternut Squash and Fennel Lasagna). But when it's raw, fennel tastes like an early May morning along the banks of the Arno.

Use a very sharp knife or, if you have it, a mandoline slicer for this dish, so you can get the thinnest possible sections of fennel and cabbage. The fennel bulb should be sliced whole for this salad, so it retains its heart-shaped outline. Buy the best balsamic vinegar and olive oil you can manage, so their flavors will quietly finish this perfect dish.

1 whole fennel bulb, sliced thin
½ head green cabbage, sliced thin
2 Tbsp. good balsamic vinegar
2 Tbsp. best extra virgin olive oil
Sea salt to taste
Freshly ground black pepper to taste

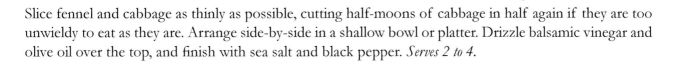

Slice fennel and cabbage as thinly as possible, cutting half-moons of cabbage in half again if they are too unwieldy to eat as they are. Arrange side-by-side in a shallow bowl or platter. Drizzle balsamic vinegar and olive oil over the top, and finish with sea salt and black pepper. *Serves 2 to 4.*

Perfect as a starter or as an accompaniment to Apricot Chutney-Glazed Salmon or Swiss-Style Lake Trout and Tiny Herbed Potatoes.

ROMAINE, CHÈVRE, AND APPLE SALAD

Goat cheese, or chèvre—which simply means "goat" in French—originated in the Loire Valley in the eighth century, after goats were first brought to the area. It is a soft, highly nutritious cheese, containing more essential vitamins and minerals than cows' milk. It also has higher levels of fatty acids and less milk proteins than cheese from cows, which makes it tangy, soft, and crumbly (and makes it easier to digest than lactose); chèvre's protein structure makes it melt differently, too, becoming creamy rather than gooey. Goat cheese has grown greatly in popularity since the eighth century, and it is now made all over the world.

This salad became our family's favorite go-to dish for those long Shabbat afternoons when we'd already had our fill of rich food at lunch. As long as the ingredients were fresh and crisp, it never let us down.

SALAD
One head romaine lettuce, chopped
1 large, very firm apple, cored and diced
3 oz. chèvre, crumbled
¼ c. coarsely chopped walnuts
¼ c. dried cranberries
Sweet Citrus Vinaigrette (see below)

Wash and gently dry lettuce before chopping. Core and dice apples small. Add nuts and dried cranberries. Crumble chèvre over salad using a fork or fingers. Toss together gently before and again after dressing.

SWEET CITRUS VINAIGRETTE
½ c. extra virgin olive oil
¼ c. red wine vinegar
2 Tbsp. fresh lemon or lime juice
1 Tbsp. honey or agave, or more to taste
¼ tsp. salt and freshly ground black pepper to taste

Combine all ingredients and whisk briskly. Use a third to half of vinaigrette for these salad proportions (or multiply easily for a larger crowd), and dress immediately before serving. *Serves 2 to 4.*

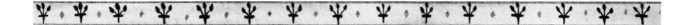

NECTARINE AND ROASTED CORN SALAD

This salad is one of my more recent inventions, and Jesse requested it specifically for this cookbook (even though it is not, strictly speaking, an old family favorite). As with anything involving fresh corn or summer stone fruit, it's a keeper—and combining these two in one dish just seals the deal.

Nectarines were developed from the single mutation of a peach, so they only differ by one gene—the one that makes nectarine skin smooth instead of fuzzy. This is the reason I prefer them to peaches. I eagerly look forward to nectarine season every year, and last summer they were the sweetest and juiciest ever. Each week at the farmer's market, I would buy more than I could eat and end up having to get creative with the fruit that got too soft. What a happy problem to solve!

SALAD

2 ears of corn, shucked, grilled or steamed
1 c. fresh cherry tomatoes, sliced in half
4 ripe nectarines, pitted and cut into chunks
½ c. feta cheese, crumbled
½ small red onion, diced very fine
Handful of fresh cilantro, chopped (optional)
Red or green leaf lettuce, optional

Grill or steam whole corn for 5 minutes. When cooled, slice the kernels off with a sharp knife and place in a medium bowl. Add halved cherry tomatoes, nectarine chunks, feta, onion, and cilantro (if using). Toss with lemon agave dressing (below). Serve on a bed of greens, if desired. *Makes about 3 to 5 servings.*

LEMON AGAVE DRESSING

¼ c. extra virgin olive oil
¼ cup fresh-squeezed lemon juice
1 Tbsp. agave nectar, more or less to taste
¼ tsp. salt and freshly ground black pepper to taste

Whisk all ingredients together. Use a third to half of dressing for salad, reserving remainder in fridge.

WATERMELON FETA SALAD WITH BLUEBERRIES AND CANDIED PISTACHIOS

This salad is like the world in a bowl. Archaeologists have traced the first pistachio seeds twenty-five hundred years back, to the Middle East. Watermelon originated either in West or Northeast Africa; its provenance and history are murky, as it crossed to Europe and then North America through colonialism and the slave trade. The blueberry is also ancient and hard to trace—it grows wild all over northern Europe, Asia, and America. The US was the first country to begin domesticating blueberries in 1908 and is still their largest producer, growing nearly 250 thousand tons a year. Feta cheese, a crumbly, brined white cheese made from curds of sheep's milk, originated in Greece. It, too, can be traced back more than two thousand years, but it wasn't until the seventeenth century that Greeks began referring to it as *feta*, meaning "slice," likely due to the practice of slicing pieces off larger blocks.

These flavors, flowing together from so many places on earth, combine beautifully in the bowl, and the notes of sweet and salty, crunchy and juicy, are just what creative cooking is all about: finding a harmonious balance that pleases many different points of the palate. I have given some loose quantities in this recipe, but really, these ingredients can be combined in any amounts. *Serves 6 to 10 as a starter, 3 to 5 as a meal.*

SALAD
2 large heads chopped romaine or 3 c. field greens
1 European or 2 Persian cucumbers
1 c. blueberries
2 c. seedless watermelon, cubed
4 oz. feta cheese
½ c. candied pistachios (see below)
¼ c. dried cranberries, or more to taste
Sweet citrus vinaigrette

Make candied pistachios first, so they have time to cool (see next page). Chop romaine lettuce. Peel and slice cucumbers, and combine with lettuce, blueberries, nuts, and dried fruit in a large bowl. Cube watermelon and crumble feta, adding these just before dressing the salad, as their weight and moisture will wilt the lettuce if allowed to sit. Toss with about half of Sweet Citrus Vinaigrette (next page) and serve.

CANDIED PISTACHIOS (OR OTHER NUTS)

2 Tbsp. butter (or margarine for nondairy)
2 - 3 Tbsp. raw or turbinado sugar
2 c. pistachios (or almonds, cashews, walnuts, etc.)

Preheat a large nonstick pan. Melt butter or margarine, then add sugar and turn down to medium low, stirring often until sugar starts to dissolve. After 2 minutes or so, add nuts and spread out in a single layer to toast, shaking the pan several times so the sugary butter coats the nuts before they finish toasting.

Stir almost constantly, watching the color deepen and being sure the nuts don't burn. When you can smell the nutty fragrance, pour the nuts out onto a plate lined with parchment paper and *don't touch until cool*. This makes about four times the amount you need for the proportions of salad listed here. When safely cooled, break clumps apart to put in salad, storing remainder in an airtight container (if you haven't eaten it all).

SWEET CITRUS VINAIGRETTE

½ c. extra virgin olive oil
¼ c. red wine vinegar
2 Tbsp. fresh lime or lemon juice
1 Tbsp. honey or agave, or more to taste
¼ tsp. salt
Freshly ground black pepper to taste

Combine all ingredients and mix well.

Use lettuce leaves to taste the dressing before you dress the salad, aiming to achieve a balance between the sour and the sweet, with enough salt to offset both. Pour about half the dressing over salad just before serving and toss, adjusting amount according to your preference. Leftover dressing keeps well at room temperature or in the refrigerator.

CARA CARA ORANGE SALAD WITH CRANBERRIES AND CARAMELIZED ONIONS

The Cara Cara orange is not only my favorite citrus fruit but the source of a great food origin story. (See Citrus Curd for more on the origins of citrus fruit.) This pink-blushed orange variety was first discovered as a spontaneously mutated bud on a Washington navel orange tree at the Hacienda Cara Cara in Valencia, Venezuela. That one blossom was cultivated, shared, and eventually spread throughout the world. I love this story for two reasons: first, it is a reminder that nature can produce miracles, not just disasters, and that we must all protect the earth's ability to continue making its own magic. Second, the flourishing of the Cara Cara strikes me as a metaphor for human parenthood: we might think we know what we are passing on when we bring children into the world, but from the moment they are born, they will surprise, confound, and thrill us again and again. If we feed and water them, give them sunlight, encouragement, and affection, they will flourish—but they will still carve their own unique paths through the world.

Cara Cara oranges didn't become widely available in the US until the early 2000s. The way I recall it, they appeared on the scene one winter in Connecticut, described as "pink oranges with hints of rose and raspberry," sitting on the shelf like a goddess among citrus fruits.

This salad is a little fussy, but it's well worth the effort. You can prepare the elements in advance, but don't assemble until just before serving, so the heavy, juicy ingredients don't wilt the greens.

SALAD
2 large sweet onions, caramelized (see below)
3 Cara Cara oranges, suprêmed (see below), juice reserved
3 c. baby lettuce or field greens
2 or 3 Persian cucumbers, sliced thin
1 large sweet red pepper, diced
½ c. shelled pistachios
½ c. dried cranberries or cherries
1 ripe avocado, optional (add just before serving)

CARAMELIZED ONIONS
2 to 3 Tbsp. extra virgin olive oil
3 large sweet onions, sliced thin
Generous pinch salt

Preheat skillet on medium-high. Add half of olive oil and allow to liquefy. Add onions. When you have a good sizzle, turn down to medium low. Add a pinch of salt and remainder of oil. Stir often and adjust temperature as necessary to achieve a nice caramel color, usually after around 30 minutes. Be patient. The onions should become very soft, golden brown, and greatly reduced in volume. Turn off heat; set aside.

SUPRÊMED (SECTIONED) ORANGES
Cut top and bottom off each orange using a sharp knife, so it stands flat on a cutting board. Cut off rind with sharp paring knife around orange, removing bitter white pith but leaving as much of the fruit as possible. Hold peeled orange over a bowl to catch juice and slice along the segment lines to get wedges of orange with no membrane. Drop the wedges into a separate container and cover. Squeeze husks of oranges into the juice bowl and use for the dressing. Don't mix oranges with greens until ready to serve.

HONEY ORANGE DRESSING
Juice from sectioned oranges (2 Tbsp. or more)
About 2 Tbsp. red wine vinegar
¼ c. extra virgin olive oil
1 Tbsp. honey
¼ tsp. salt
Freshly ground black pepper to taste

Whisk all ingredients until blended. This recipe makes more dressing than you'll need.

Place lettuce, sliced peppers, and cucumbers in a large salad bowl. Add pistachios and dried cranberries. Add caramelized onions and oranges just before serving, and toss gently with about a third of dressing, adjusting amount as needed. Arrange avocado slices around edges of bowl, if desired, and drizzle with a little dressing. Serve immediately. *Serves 6 to 8 as a starter, 3 to 5 as a meal.* See the cover of this cookbook for a luscious illustration of this much-loved salad.

ISRAELI BREAKFAST SALAD BUFFET

I finally made it to Israel for the first time when I was forty, and by then, I had heard so much about it that I thought nothing would surprise me. But there were so many surprises! The range and beauty of the landscape in that tiny country, from the Negev Desert to the shores of Tel Aviv to the Galilee Mountains; the interweaving of ancient and modern through every facet of society; the stunning assortment of markets and street foods that turned every other corner into a feast for the eyes and mouth.

As a cook, the single most revolutionary thing I took away from Israel was salad for breakfast. In retrospect, it makes perfect sense that Israelis would start their day with the bounty of the land; the fresh fruits and vegetables are plentiful there and represent something of an agricultural coup in the desert climate. It wasn't just the emblematic Israeli salad of tomatoes, cucumbers, onions, and peppers; it was this concoction combined with other delights—the creamiest hummus, soft and hard cheeses, olives, salty nuts, warm pita, and local honey—that made for such a memorable breakfast.

Get the freshest ingredients you can for this meal. Nothing is cooked (except the chickpeas), so you can really taste each element. Hummus is a dip made out of ground chickpeas and tahini, a sesame paste that can be found in most well-stocked stores these days. Prepared hummus is ubiquitous now, of course, but it's also very easy to make at home and tastes extra wonderful when fresh. My Poppi loved to make his own hummus and I have tried to faithfully recreate his recipe below. Adjusting the balance of garlic, tahini, salt, and lemon will shift the prevailing flavors of the hummus quite a bit. Experiment with the recipe until it tastes right to you. Or, if fresh hummus is a bridge too far, just skip it and buy a container at the market. I've listed a number of my personal favorite accompaniments for this special meal, but I'm sure you will come up with your own assortment to harmonize for a blowout breakfast salad buffet of your own.

ISRAELI SALAD

1 European cucumber or 3 Persians, diced small
2 large, ripe tomatoes, diced small
2 sweet bell peppers, diced small
¼ red onion, minced
Juice of 1 lemon, or more to taste
3 Tbsp. extra virgin olive oil, or more if adding extra lemon
1 tsp. dried oregano
½ tsp. salt, or more to taste
Freshly ground black pepper to taste

Combine diced vegetables in a glass bowl. Add lemon juice and olive oil, adjusting amounts as desired. Sprinkle with salt, pepper, and oregano, and toss to coat. Taste to adjust salt and pepper if needed.

HUMMUS

¼ c. tahini, stirred well before measuring
2 Tbsp. extra virgin olive oil, plus extra for serving
½ tsp. ground cumin (fresh jar if possible)
½ tsp. salt, or more to taste
2 cloves garlic, minced
15 oz. can chickpeas, drained and rinsed, or 1½ c. home-cooked
Fresh juice of 1 lemon
2 Tbsp. ice cold water or more as needed
Ground paprika for serving

Blend for full amount of time for each step in this recipe to achieve creamy texture.

Place tahini in a food processor and blend for 30 seconds. Stop machine, scrape down sides with a rubber spatula, and blend for another 30 to 60 seconds, until the tahini is light and creamy-looking. Add olive oil, cumin, salt, and garlic, and blend for another 30 seconds. Add the chickpeas and lemon juice and blend for 60 seconds, scraping down the sides of the bowl when you stop. Repeat as needed for up to 2 more minutes to achieve a thick, smooth paste.

Scrape down sides again and turn food processor back on, pouring in 2 Tbsp. water and blending until desired creamy consistency is achieved, adding a bit more water if needed. Taste and adjust salt, and blend one more time. When the hummus looks right to you, place it in a wide, shallow bowl and smooth the top with the rubber spatula. Sprinkle with paprika and drizzle with extra virgin olive oil.

Place bowls of Israeli salad and hummus in the center of your table, and surround with other bowls, platters, or plates of complementary foods, such as:

Warm pita bread
Whole grain crackers
Soft hard-boiled eggs (see Salade Niçoise for directions)
Mediterranean olives, like Kalamata or Niçoise
Greek or Israeli feta, cut into chunks
Small curd and/or whipped cottage cheese
Hard and semi-soft cheeses, like Gouda, manchego, cheddar, fontina
Good quality honey, preferably local
Any flavor jam, fruit spread, or fruit compote (I like apricot best)
Nuts such as pistachios, macadamias, cashews, and walnuts
Dried fruits such as apricots, yellow raisins, and dates
Fresh fruits such as figs, oranges, and melons

Invite everyone to build their own breakfast. Can also be served for lunch, and would do very nicely for hors d'oeuvres at a party or festive dinner. *This meal is expandable, serving from 4 to 6 upward.* Have fun with it!

CREAMY CURRIED CHICKEN SALAD

This is my version of a dish I first encountered when I was seventeen and working at a gourmet shop in New Haven. Their creamy curried chicken salad was a favorite with customers and became my go-to lunch. It was a cold spin on a Swiss dish I remembered from childhood, made with curried chicken and fruit toppings (see Creamy Vegetable Curry with Grand Fixings). It took me decades to circle back to it, and plenty of trial and error to find the right balance of flavors; the end result is surprising and wonderful.

SALAD

3 skin-on chicken breasts (prepared as below)
1 c. firm red grapes, halved
2 apples, cored and chopped
Large handful walnuts, roughly broken
3 stalks celery, chopped
½ c. golden raisins
¼ c. dried cranberries
Large handful fresh cilantro, chopped

Preheat oven to 450 degrees. Place chicken breasts in a baking pan, cover with foil, and roast until juices run clear, 30 to 40 minutes. While chicken is cooling, prepare remaining ingredients above and combine in a large bowl. Skin chicken and shred into chunks. Add to bowl, tossing with curry dressing to coat all ingredients. Allow flavors to marry for 30 minutes. Toss again right before serving (dressing settles).

CREAMY CURRY DRESSING

½ c. mayonnaise
¼ c. cashew, almond, or other vegan sour cream
½ c. cashew, almond, or other nondairy milk
2 Tbsp. agave nectar or honey
¼ to ½ tsp. salt, to taste
1 tsp. mild curry powder

Whisk all ingredients until smooth and golden. Pour over salad, tossing well to coat. *Serves 6 to 8.*

SALADE NIÇOISE WITH SESAME-CRUSTED TUNA

As its name suggests, Salade Niçoise (pronounced "nee-SWAHZ") originated in the city of Nice, located in the French Riviera. Called *la salada nissarda* in the local Niçard dialect, it was originally served to fishermen when they returned from their catch. The unique flavors of the traditional niçoise bring together many of the region's culinary pleasures: briny Niçoise olives, vine-ripened tomatoes, sunny hard-boiled eggs, and spring onions, crowned with canned tuna or anchovies. Like many dishes with humble beginnings, over time it has been adopted as a darling of the culinary world. My version of Salade Niçoise with pan-roasted haricots verts and tiny steamed potatoes reflects a variation that has become common over the last hundred years. I like to add sweet bell peppers, too, and serve it on a bed of baby greens.

My use of sesame-crusted tuna steaks is not, strictly speaking, in keeping with traditional Niçoise, but they are the crown jewels of this salad. They should only be cooked for a few short moments to preserve their tenderness and red hue. The addition of sesame seeds creates a tiny barrier that allows you an extra minute of pan-searing to warm the steaks through before they have to be rushed off the skillet. If tuna steaks are unavailable or out of reach, you can, of course, use anchovies, sardines, or canned tuna in their place; try to get the kind in olive oil, as it has a richer flavor. It won't be quite as decadent, but it will be all the more authentic! And if you can't get haricots verts, conventional green beans will do—just try to get ones that are thin, firm, and light green. (See Haricots Verts with Toasted Onions for more about French green beans.) The potatoes and eggs can be prepared a few hours or a day ahead, but cook the green beans and the tuna right before serving, and don't assemble anything until the tuna is done.

This dish might look extraordinarily involved, but because each element cooks quickly, and some can be made at the same time, it takes well under an hour from start to finish.

Remove tuna steaks from fridge as you are making the other components of the salad, so that they reach room temperature by the time you are ready to cook them (last, just before assembling salad).

SALADE NIÇOISE

4 eggs, soft-hardboiled (see below)
8 oz. tiny new potatoes, boiled
8 oz. haricots verts (or green beans), pan roasted
2 cloves garlic, minced
2 large tuna steaks (1½ - 2 lbs. total), very fresh
3 - 4 Tbsp. toasted sesame seeds
Onion salt, sea salt, and black pepper to taste
¼ c. extra virgin olive oil (for elements below), more as needed
About 2 - 3 c. baby greens
1 pint cherry tomatoes or 2 medium tomatoes, diced
1 orange bell pepper
½ c. Niçoise or Kalamata olives

Simple Lemon Vinaigrette (below)

Prepare elements of salad as instructed below. See directions after Simple Lemon Vinaigrette to assemble.

SOFT-HARDBOILED EGGS

Place eggs in small saucepan with enough water to cover. Bring to a boil, keeping your eye on the pot (it will boil, I promise). As soon as it reaches a rolling boil, take pot off the heat. Cover tightly and set a timer for exactly 9 minutes. When time is up, run eggs immediately under cold water until they are no longer too hot to peel. Remove shells under running water with care; yolks may not be totally solid (perfectly fine if eggs are fresh). Set aside.

NEW POTATOES

Place potatoes in saucepan with enough water to cover. Bring to a boil, turn down, and simmer until just soft, 15 to 20 minutes. Drain potatoes, toss with 1 Tbsp. olive oil, onion salt, and pepper. Set aside.

PAN-ROASTED HARICOTS VERTS

Trim beans so no hard tails remain. Heat a large skillet on high, adding 1 Tbsp. olive oil when hot. Add haricots verts and brown on one side for 3 to 5 minutes; stir to turn over and repeat, turning down heat to medium high. Add minced garlic, stirring often to prevent from burning. Remove beans when still a bit crisp and bright green. Sprinkle generously with sea salt and black pepper. Set aside.

SESAME-CRUSTED TUNA STEAKS

Preheat skillet on high and add 2 Tbsp. olive oil. While oil heats up, prepare tuna steaks. Place steaks between two paper towels on a plate, pressing down to drain any remaining moisture just before cooking. Remove paper towels. Sprinkle sesame seeds into both sides of fish, sprinkle liberally with onion salt, and add a couple of grinds black pepper. Place tuna carefully in hot oil, searing on first side for 1 to 2 minutes depending on thickness. Turn steaks over and sear for only 1 minute on second side. Sesame seeds on outside of tuna should be crusted on and browned. Take steaks off the pan while there is still a bright red strip of uncooked tuna through the center. Place on a cutting board and allow to cool while dressing salad.

Slice seared tuna steaks on the bias—in the opposite direction to their natural segmentation—so slices remain intact. (Tuna steaks can also be served as a fast, elegant entrée.)

SIMPLE LEMON VINAIGRETTE

Juice of 1 lemon
1 Tbsp. red wine vinegar
¼ c. extra virgin olive oil
¼ tsp. sea salt, or more to taste
Freshly ground black pepper to taste

Whisk ingredients together until blended. Mix again just before dressing salad.

Place greens in a large, shallow bowl or a deep platter. Cut cherry tomatoes in half and add. Toss greens and tomatoes with about half of lemon vinaigrette. Cut hard-boiled eggs in half the long way to create ovals. Slice orange pepper into strips, and arrange with potatoes, green beans, eggs, and olives in neat stacks on top of greens around sides of bowl. Arrange tuna slices in center, leaning them neatly against each other. Drizzle second half of dressing over cooked ingredients. Bring to the table and take a bow.
Serves 3 to 5.

COOKING TIPS TO LIVE BY

PREHEATING POTS

In this cookbook, I often suggest preheating your skillet or soup pot, then adding olive oil or butter and allowing it to "liquefy." This makes sense with butter, but you might wonder what I mean when it comes to oil, since it is already a liquid. But if you try it, you'll see that once it hits the heat, the oil looks thinner and becomes somewhat runny, and then it begins to shimmer just a little. That's when you should add the food, because when the oil gets hot enough, it creates a shell with the natural proteins in the food. This will prevent the rest of the oil from soaking in and making the food taste greasy. That said, if oil goes beyond the shimmer point, it will begin to smoke, and then it releases unhealthy free radicals that are best to avoid.

HEAVY-BOTTOM PANS

In some of these recipes, I recommend the use of a heavy-bottom skillet or saucepan. This is because the heavier base will retain the heat of the stove and distribute it more evenly than a lightweight one. If you are able to make any investments for your cooking adventures, high quality cookware is second only to a good sharp knife.

THE IMPORTANCE OF SALT

Salt is an essential ingredient in many of my recipes, especially the baked goods. In the proper quantity, salt acts as an intensifier for every flavor, but like any seasoning, it can be overused, as it is in many processed foods. Too much salt—like too much sugar—is not only unhealthy but pointless, as it can overwhelm all of the flavors it is meant to enhance. But the thoughtful addition of salt is crucial, and with baking in particular, it can transform a dish from cloying or bland to perfectly balanced and delightful.

COOK AHEAD

I am a big fan of making food in advance, both for convenience and to allow you to enjoy your own handiwork. It is no fun to sit down at the table exhausted, sweaty, and irritable; especially with larger meals, I recommend you make whatever you can ahead of time. This principle grew out of my Sabbath-observant years, when the food for both the Friday evening and Saturday meals had to be cooked before sundown on Friday. In this cookbook, I have tried to point out opportunities for cooking ahead wherever possible. I recommend you read all the way through the instructions before you begin, so you can plan accordingly. I have found cooking ahead to be an invaluable skill: it allows you to keep clean-up under control, spread out the time you spend on your feet, and enjoy the food you worked so hard to put on the table.

ENTRÉES

SPANISH OMELET

I had never tasted a Spanish omelet until I traveled to Barcelona for the first time in 2013. I stayed at the Hotel Pulitzer—which I had chosen mostly for its name since, at the time, I was preparing to finish my creative writing MFA. The hotel turned out to be a beautiful refuge on a side street off the colorful main boulevard, Las Ramblas. The interior was all glowing wood and billowing white curtains, and breakfast on the covered patio was fabulous: every day, they served delectable pastries, fragrant dark coffee, meats and cheeses, and Spanish omelet, a savory *torta* of eggs, potatoes, and onions.

There is dispute about the exact origin of Spanish omelet or *tortilla de patatas*—and whether it originally contained onion—but it first surfaced at the end of the eighteenth century during a period of widespread hunger, when it became popular for being nutritious, cheap, and filling. It's true that it is a very budget-friendly dish, but don't be fooled: the sum of this omelet is far greater than its parts. Do plan ahead, because this baby takes about an hour to make! Is it worth it? Absolutely. *A light meal for 4 to 6.*

¼ to ½ c. extra virgin olive oil
2 onions, sliced into ¼ to ½ inch rings
5 - 6 yellow potatoes, peeled
10 - 12 eggs, beaten
½ to 1 tsp. salt, or more to taste
Freshly ground black pepper to taste
Crème fraiche or sour cream to serve

Preheat a deep, wide skillet on medium-high and add 2 Tbsp. oil. Add onions, allowing to soften and begin browning, 10 minutes. Slice peeled potatoes ¼ to ½ inch thick and add to skillet with some of salt, then pour oil all over potatoes, at least 2 Tbsp. more (enough oil is crucial to recipe). Turn and combine with spatula. Cook on medium-low until potatoes are soft but not mushy, about 20 minutes, turning over often so they brown but don't burn. When done, press potatoes and onions into an even layer in skillet.

Beat eggs with more salt and pepper, and pour over potato mixture to cover. Cook 20 to 25 min., increasing heat a bit if needed, using a rubber spatula to retract edges a few times so runny eggs reach heat. When omelet looks mostly set, release sides and bottom with spatula, cover tightly with a platter, and flip. Slide back into skillet to finish (3 to 5 min.), then re-platter. Serve in wedges with crème fraiche or sour cream.

CHÈVRE AND SQUASH BLOSSOM FRITTATA

Squash blossoms are the delicate, edible orange-yellow flowers that grow with several varieties of squash. They are used extensively in Mediterranean, Latin, and Indigenous cuisines, often fried or stuffed with soft cheese. Here, they are cooked into a frittata, a large Italian omelet in which eggs are mixed with other elements before setting, rather than being folded over them afterward. This light and beautiful recipe was inspired by a chef I met in Verona, Italy. He and his wife ran a charming B & B, and every morning, he would astound us with breakfast feasts that included savory dishes like this one, and sweet ones like tiramisu made with espresso and fresh cream—the height of decadence for breakfast. He made his frittata with Gorgonzola, which I don't usually love, but the flavors were so mild and fresh that I adored it. In my recipe, I have substituted chèvre (goat cheese), which also pairs well with the squash blossoms; if you prefer Gorgonzola, have at it! *Makes 4 to 6 light servings.*

2 Tbsp. extra virgin olive oil
½ large sweet onion, chopped small
3 scallions, green and white parts, chopped
8 squash blossoms, stems removed
1 Tbsp. butter
½ tsp. salt and freshly ground black pepper to taste
8 large eggs, whisked
3 oz. chèvre, crumbled, plus more for garnish

Preheat a nonstick skillet to medium-high and add oil. Add chopped onion and scallion; reduce heat to medium and sauté until soft but not brown, about 8 minutes. Gently rinse and dry squash blossoms, pinching off stems. Melt butter in skillet and add squash blossoms, sautéing about 30 seconds. Turn off heat, sprinkle with ¼ tsp. salt, and gently but artfully arrange blossoms in the shape of a flower in the pan.

Beat eggs lightly and stir in crumbled chèvre, remaining salt, and pepper. Turn heat to medium. Pour egg mixture into skillet and as it begins to set, use a rubber spatula to retract sides of frittata so uncooked eggs can get to heat. When eggs are mostly set (10 to 15 minutes), run spatula gently around sides and under frittata to loosen. Hold a platter tightly on top of skillet and flip so frittata drops out. Slide back into skillet on other side and allow to set completely, about 5 minutes. Re-platter; sprinkle with extra chèvre to serve.

SUMMER CORN TART

Summer in America would not be complete without fresh corn on the cob. It's best at the height of its seasonal sweetness, grilled or boiled, then rolled in butter and sprinkled with salt. Corn, or *maize*, is native to Mexico. Over two thousand years ago, it spread widely across North and South America and became firmly entrenched as a staple of the Indigenous diet. Corn and cream are complementary flavors that heighten each other to great effect (see also New England Corn Chowder). This dish is another Euro-American hybrid, combining native summer corn with the flavors of a classic French soufflé and the sweet/savory balance of a kugel. Serve this tart any time as a light meal or as an accompaniment to fish. *Serves 3 to 5 as a main dish.*

3 Tbsp. butter, divided
3 ears corn, steamed (or 3 c. frozen, thawed and drained)
5 large eggs, beaten
2 Tbsp. raw sugar
2 Tbsp. cornstarch, sifted
8 scallions, chopped, or 1 red onion, diced small
1½ c. whole milk
½ c. heavy cream
1½ c. grated sharp cheddar
1 tsp. salt
Freshly ground black pepper to taste

Preheat oven to 350 degrees. Butter a deep-dish pie pan and set aside. Shuck corn and cook for 5 minutes in a pot of boiling water. Remove and allow to cool. Cut ends off cobs so they stand flat when vertical. Shear corn off cobs with a sharp knife. Set aside. Combine eggs and sugar in a bowl, whisking until well blended. Sift cornstarch over egg mixture (to avoid lumps) and whisk until smooth.

Preheat a skillet. Add 1 Tbsp. butter and sauté scallions/onions 5 to 7 minutes until soft. Add remaining butter to melt, then pour contents of skillet into bowl of egg mixture. Whisk in milk and cream; add cheddar, corn, salt, and pepper. Stir to combine. Pour into prepared pan and bake in center of oven for 45 to 50 minutes, until top is golden and tart is just solid in center. Cool 15 minutes before serving.

ROYAL VEGETABLE LASAGNA

Oh, lasagna. The king of casseroles, the queen of comfort foods. It's not something you make every day, so you want it to be special. The key to a really good lasagna is, well, everything. It's important that you use whole milk ricotta if you can, so the creaminess provides contrast with the acidity of the tomatoes. If you can't get it, lowfat ricotta or 4 percent cottage cheese will do. I don't recommend fat free ricotta or cottage cheese, as they're full of thickeners to make up for the missing fat and can affect the taste of your lasagna.

Some might call it sacrilege, but I am a big fan of "oven-ready" (also called "no boil") lasagna noodles, as they are thinner and lighter than conventional ones, and you won't have to cook, drain, and separate them. Simply assemble your lasagna with the dry pasta sheets and cover the pan tightly, letting the sauce cook them in the oven. Of course, if you desire the more traditional noodles, they are fine, too.

Speaking of sacrilege, my shortcut red sauce brings a bright tomato flavor to this recipe with a fraction of the prep time. That said, I recommend you avoid the further shortcut of prepared jarred sauces, which often have additives and do not taste as fresh as simple canned tomatoes. If you already make homemade tomato sauce, by all means use that. But the shortcut sauce works well here. As for the vegetables: below is my favorite combination, but there are many others that would taste lovely. Whatever you choose, be sure to sauté the veggies and drain them well so they don't make your lasagna watery.

Finally, it is crucial to use a generous amount of good quality Parmesan and mozzarella cheeses, especially on top. (For more on Parmigiano Reggiano, see Serena's "Noonies.") Now, *basta!* On with the task at hand.

LASAGNA ELEMENTS
2 boxes oven-ready lasagna noodles (18 sheets)
Spinach ricotta mixture (see below)
1 batch shortcut red sauce (see below)
Veggie mixture of zucchini, onions, mushrooms (see below)
3 c. freshly grated mozzarella, more to taste
1 c. freshly grated Parmesan (pref. Parmigiano Reggiano) for top, more to taste

Follow directions for each element of lasagna below. Assemble according to instructions at end of recipe.

SPINACH RICOTTA MIXTURE
1 lb. ricotta cheese, pref. whole milk
½ c. freshly grated Parmigiano Reggiano
About 6 oz. baby spinach
1 handful fresh basil leaves
2 eggs, lightly beaten
2 good shakes garlic powder
½ tsp. salt and freshly ground black pepper

Mix ricotta cheese in bowl with Parmesan. Steam spinach for 1 to 2 minutes to wilt. Cool slightly, pressing out moisture in a colander. Chop spinach and add to ricotta mixture. Chiffonade basil leaves (roll into a tube and cut across to get ribbons of basil). Add to bowl with remaining ingredients. Mix well. Set aside.

SHORTCUT RED SAUCE*
2 28-oz. cans crushed tomatoes
Handful basil leaves, chiffonaded
1 tsp. dried basil
1 tsp. dried oregano
2 cloves garlic, minced
1 Tbsp. agave nectar or honey
½ tsp. salt, or more to taste
Freshly ground black pepper to taste

Pour crushed tomatoes into large bowl. Add fresh and dried basil, oregano, garlic, and agave or honey. Mix thoroughly and taste. Add salt and pepper as needed for robust flavor. No need to cook this sauce—it will roast for 90 minutes in the oven once the lasagna is assembled. Set aside.

*If you are feeling extra-ambitious and want to make your own red sauce from scratch, see recipe for Cheese and Tomato Vidalia Pie. Follow directions for "Tomato Filling," doubling quantities of tomatoes, garlic, and basil. Cook according to directions, adding dried herbs and agave from short-cut sauce above, but don't fully reduce sauce—it doesn't need to be as thick for the lasagna. You will need 6 cups of sauce, so keep this in mind as you go, and be ready to supplement with canned crushed tomatoes if necessary.

VEGGIE MIXTURE

1 large sweet onion, diced
2 zucchinis, diced
1 lb. cremini or white mushrooms, sliced
3 Tbsp. extra virgin olive oil
3 cloves garlic, minced
Salt and freshly ground black pepper to taste

Preheat oven to 350 degrees while you prepare veggies. Dice onion and zucchini, and slice mushrooms, keeping each vegetable separate. Preheat a large skillet or soup pot, add 2 Tbsp. olive oil, and allow to heat briefly. Add onions, cooking and stirring until they turn translucent, then turn heat down to medium and continue cooking until onions are soft and beginning to brown, about 15 minutes. Add zucchini, sautéing until bright green, about 5 minutes. Add mushrooms, garlic, and remaining Tbsp. olive oil and sauté until garlic is fragrant and mushrooms have released their liquid, about 10 more minutes. Season mixture well with salt and pepper. Set veggies aside in a colander with a bowl underneath so they drain as you assemble.

ASSEMBLING LASAGNA

In large casserole dish (at least 9 x 13 in.), spread out one or two ladles of sauce just to cover bottom. Line up 3 sheets of oven-ready lasagna horizontally to form a single layer. Spread with a third of spinach ricotta mixture. Press down on sautéed veggies in colander to release liquid and spoon a third onto ricotta, spreading to cover. Add 3 more lasagna sheets, spread on a third of red sauce, then sprinkle with a third of mozzarella. Repeat process twice more (as below). Finish with at least 1 c. freshly grated Parmesan.

1. Sauce base (so bottom layer of noodles doesn't dry out)
2. Noodles, ricotta mixture, veggie mixture
3. Noodles, red sauce, mozzarella cheese
4. Repeat steps 2 and 3 twice more each, for six layers, topping last with Parmesan.

Place lasagna pan on a cookie sheet. Oil one side of a long piece of foil, crimp tightly over lasagna, and place in oven for 1 hour. Remove foil and bake, uncovered, for an additional 30 minutes, until noodles look soft, cheese is beginning to brown, and sauce is merrily bubbling at the edges. If cheese gets too dark before sauce begins bubbling, loosely tent lasagna with foil again. Remove from oven and wait 15 minutes to serve. Perfectly complemented by an All-Green Salad with Classic French Vinaigrette. *Serves 8 to 10.*

BUTTERNUT SQUASH AND FENNEL LASAGNA

The Kripalu Yoga Center in Lenox, Massachusetts, has been a favorite haunt of mine for decades. The combination of peace, indulgence, and incredible food at this monastery-turned-retreat-center is always just what I need. On one of my most interesting visits, I took a cooking class with the Kripalu chefs and learned some of the reasons why the food there is so excellent: it is unfailingly fresh, local, and seasonal.

This lasagna, inspired by a recipe in the *Kripalu Winter Cookbook,* is surprising in several ways. In place of red sauce, it has a bechamel, known in Italy as *besciamella*—a rich white sauce that provides a silky, creamy base for this dish, which does not contain ricotta, classic spices, or meat, either. What it does contain is butternut squash, a gourd native to the Americas, and fennel, an ancient Mediterranean plant that tastes ever so slightly of licorice and adds a unique twist of flavor. The original Kripalu recipe only calls for fennel seeds, but my version uses the whole fennel bulb, roasted at high heat to caramelize it, revealing a light, spring-like flavor that acts as the perfect foil to the wintery butternut squash. This happy marriage of flavors seems to keep repeating itself in my kitchen—and now in yours, too.

Make separate elements of lasagna first, then assemble according to instructions on the following page.

BUTTERNUT SQUASH AND FENNEL FILLING
1 large or 2 medium butternut squashes, cubed
2 fresh fennel bulbs, diced, fronds reserved
2 Tbsp. extra virgin olive oil
1 tsp. cinnamon
1 tsp. sea salt, or more to taste
Freshly ground black pepper to taste
1 Tbsp. fresh thyme (or 1 tsp. dried)

Preheat oven to 450 degrees. If starting with whole squash, pierce with a fork and microwave just until soft enough to peel and cube easily, 8 to 10 minutes. Cool for a half hour, peel, scoop out seeds, then cut into 2-inch cubes. Toss with diced fennel (reserving fronds), olive oil, cinnamon, salt, and pepper. Roast on a baking sheet for 20 to 40 minutes until soft and golden. When done, sprinkle with more salt, thyme, and fennel fronds, and use a fork or potato masher to break down squash, leaving it somewhat chunky.

BECHAMEL

6 c. whole milk
½ tsp. salt
Pinch white pepper
½ c. unsalted butter
½ c. unbleached all-purpose flour

Warm milk, salt, and pepper in a saucepan at medium heat, watching carefully so the milk does not burn. When milk begins to steam and bubbles appear, turn to low, just to keep hot. Place a large skillet or second saucepan on medium heat. Add butter to melt. Add flour and whisk vigorously until it comes together as a roux (a thick paste). Let it bubble for one minute, stirring often. Add in a cup of seasoned milk a little at a time, whisking constantly. Roux will seize up at first and might form lumps, but continue whisking while pouring milk, and mixture will gradually thin and smooth out. Once it is thin enough to pour, add it back to saucepan with remaining milk, stirring until sauce thickens again, about 5 minutes. It's ready when it leaves an opaque coating on a wooden spoon. If cooled for later assembly, sauce will thicken a lot; reheat gently before assembling lasagna, whisking in a bit more milk until desired consistency is reached again.

LASAGNA

1 recipe bechamel (above)
1 box oven-ready lasagna sheets
Butternut squash and fennel filling (above)
3 c. grated mozzarella, or more to taste
½ c. grated Parmesan, or more to taste

Turn oven down to 350 degrees. Assemble lasagna in large baking dish (at least 9 x 13 in.) starting with a thin layer of bechamel. Line up 3 lasagna sheets sideways, spread out a layer of mashed squash and fennel, add another layer of noodles, cover with a layer of bechamel and sprinkle with shredded mozzarella. Alternate layers, aiming for 3 of each (but a total of 4 substantial layers is better than 6 thin ones). Sprinkle Parmesan on top of last layer of mozzarella. Cover tightly with oiled foil and cook until cheese and bechamel start to bubble, about 35 to 45 minutes. Uncover and continue baking for 5 to 10 minutes so top browns slightly. Don't let it dry out. Remove from oven and wait 10 minutes before serving in mid-sized squares (it's rich!). Fabulous for a festive late-winter meal, as a main dish alongside Cara Cara Orange Salad with Cranberries and Caramelized Onions, or with Apricot Chutney-Glazed Salmon. *Serves about 6 to 10.*

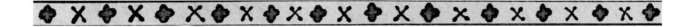

PASTA PUTTANESCA

Pasta Puttanesca is relatively modern within the canon of Italian sauces, but it came by its name, "whore's pasta," through circumstances as old as human history. The dish is said to have been invented by Italian women who became prostitutes to support themselves and their families during World War II, when their fathers, husbands, and sons were away fighting, and food was extremely scarce. The ingredients— tomatoes, hot peppers, olives, capers, and anchovies—might sound gourmet to us, but they were cheap and readily available in post-war Naples, where this sauce is thought to have originated. Legend has it that those who were truly hard hit and couldn't afford even the anchovies would put a rock from the sea into their sauce instead, to achieve the salty, briny flavor that is the hallmark of puttanesca sauce.

This is one of those dishes I never would have thought to make when I was young, because black olives, anchovies, and capers were simply not in my vocabulary yet. But my palate has shifted dramatically as I've gotten older, and now I can't think of anything more thrilling and satisfying than this super-intense, mouth-watering, and slightly spicy sauce.

As with any folk dish, this one has a thousand tiny variations. My own recipe came about through dedicated trial and error with the help of my wonderful friend, Jeremy, with whom I traveled to Italy on my most recent trip, and who has been my partner in cooking on many happy occasions.

This pasta should be served hot and fresh, preferably in a big, beautiful ceramic pasta bowl. I guarantee it will transport you straight to *Italia*.

3 Tbsp. extra virgin olive oil
6 cloves garlic, minced
About 1 oz. (half a tube) anchovy paste
About 3 Tbsp. (half a can) tomato paste
Pinch red pepper flakes
3 Tbsp. water
3 large, soft tomatoes, diced
3 large sprigs fresh basil (or 1 tsp. dried)
Generous pinch sugar
3 Tbsp. capers
½ c. Kalamata olives, sliced in half the long way
12 oz. linguine, cooked until just al dente
Grated Parmigiano Reggiano for serving

Set a large pot of heavily salted water to boil for pasta. (It should taste almost like the ocean, but not quite.)

Preheat a heavy-bottom skillet, add 2 Tbsp. olive oil, and heat briefly. Add garlic, anchovy paste, tomato paste, red pepper flakes, and water, whisking to combine. Add diced fresh tomatoes and simmer for a few minutes until they begin to break down, stirring occasionally. Chiffonade basil (roll it up tightly and slice across roll to make ribbons), and add with the sugar, turning down heat. Simmer, uncovered, until tomatoes have turned a paler, almost orange color and are reduced by half, about 7 to 10 minutes. Stir again and turn down to low, keeping warm while cooking pasta.

Cook linguine until just al dente. When pasta is almost ready, return to the sauce, turning it up slightly until just bubbling again. Add capers and olives, stirring to combine.

Drain pasta and put in a wide, shallow bowl. Pour puttanesca sauce directly on pasta and use tongs to mix and turn repeatedly until pasta is fully coated.

Serve right away with grated Parmesan cheese. (For more on Parmigiano Reggiano, see Serena's "Noonies.") Pairs brilliantly with an All-Green Salad with Classic French Vinaigrette, and begs for an Italian red wine like a Sorai or Valpolicella, or any hearty red that can stand up to the sauce's robust flavors. *Serves 3 to 5.*

PASTA AL LIMONE

This recipe was given to me by the chef at Hotel La Minerva, a little gem of an inn run by three brothers on the island of Capri. I can vividly remember the first time I tasted this dish: I was sitting on a patio inlaid with handmade Italian tiles, looking out over the gorgeous island covered with citrus trees, the Tyrrhenian Sea in the distance. For lunch, one of the brothers brought me this pasta, curled up inside a hollowed-out lemon—and from the first bite, the flavors of cream, citrus, and fresh Parmigiano burst in my mouth. It couldn't have been simpler, but sometimes those are the best dishes. I begged for the recipe and the chef generously shared it with me. When making Pasta al Limone, use the freshest possible ingredients—there are only five of them, integrated into the directions below. *Serves 2 to 3 as a small entrée or as a side with fish.*

Here is the chef's recipe, word for word, with my notes in brackets:

"Cook the pasta (Italian way…not too much). [Cook **8 oz. spaghetti** in heavily salted water until barely al dente.]

"Prepare in the pan (but no fire and no heat for now) some butter, juice of half a big lemon, finely grated skin of a lemon (just the yellow part, not the white one because very bitter), and some cream (about 100 gr. per person). [Place **2 Tbsp. butter, 1 c. heavy cream** in a skillet. Use a microplane to add **zest of one lemon** without the pith. Squeeze in **juice of half the lemon**. Warm briefly, just until butter melts, stirring to combine.]

"Once the pasta is cooked, save some "cooking water" and put the pasta in the pan. Put the heat on and go until ready. If cooking in the pan pasta is drying up…add some of the cooking water. Enjoy it!" [Place the **cooked pasta** in the skillet and turn up heat, adding **cooking water** if it gets too dry. Stir with lemon cream until cream thickens.]

Serve immediately with **freshly grated Parmigiano Reggiano**. For a festive and beautiful small plate, try La Minerva's trick of hollowing out a couple of lemon halves and winding the pasta inside them.

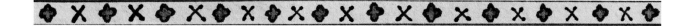

CORN AND TOMATO LINGUINE

This is one of my favorite Euro-American hybrids—and a naturally vegan one at that—combining corn and tomatoes native to the Americas with the pasta and olive oil that are Italy's stock-in-trade. Basil, which also features here, did not originate in Italy, but was likely brought over from India by Alexander the Great.

Most delicious when corn and tomatoes are in season, this dish can also be quite wonderful with frozen or canned ingredients; and dried basil will do if fresh is not available. The key is to use enough fat to coat the pasta, and to scoop up the corn, tomato, and onion from the bottom of the pasta bowl with each serving. If you're not going vegan, the salty, sharp flavor of really good Parmesan will also add a lot to this dish.

12 oz. linguine, al dente
3 Tbsp. extra virgin olive oil
2 large, sweet onions (like Vidalia)
3 ears corn (or 2 c. frozen)
Handful fresh basil, chiffonaded (or 1 tsp. dried)
1 lb. cherry tomatoes, halved (or 2 - 3 tomatoes, diced)
1 Tbsp. butter (or additional Tbsp. olive oil)
Salt and freshly ground black pepper to taste
Freshly grated Parmesan cheese for serving, optional

Set a large pot of heavily salted water to boil for pasta. In a preheated skillet, heat 2 Tbsp. olive oil on medium-high. Add onions and sauté for 10 to 15 minutes, until soft and beginning to caramelize. Cut corn off cobs with a sharp knife and add to skillet with basil, salt, and pepper. Cook until tender, 6 to 8 minutes.

Cook linguine until just al dente. As soon as pasta goes into pot, return to skillet, adjusting heat to medium-high. Add another Tbsp. olive oil and tomatoes to corn mixture, and sauté until tomatoes are just beginning to break down and oil is tinted red, 5 to 7 minutes. Add butter or more oil and stir to combine.

Drain pasta and place in a wide, shallow bowl, adding corn and tomato mixture and tossing thoroughly to coat. Taste and adjust salt and pepper. Serve immediately, passing around the freshly grated Parmigiano (if serving), and making sure to dig under the pasta for the corn and tomato treasure. *Serves 3 to 5.*

GREEN GODDESS PASTA

Pesto can be traced back to sixteenth-century Genoa, Italy, where basil, garlic, pine nuts, Parmesan, and olive oil were first mashed together in a pestle, creating this intensely flavored sauce. (For more on Parmigiano Reggiano, see Serena's "Noonies.") Though my relationship with Italy and its bright flavors certainly dates back to my childhood, I discovered the joys of pesto later in life, through my oldest friend, Miranda. We met when we were eight years old, both feeling displaced in the small Connecticut town to which our families had just moved; she had come from Brooklyn which, as she is fond of saying, was as much of a different country as Switzerland from the place where we now lived. We began a lifelong friendship then, and though our paths diverged for a time, we found ourselves, as young mothers, once again living in the same place. So our children grew up together, too, and we shared hundreds of meals, many of them featuring pasta and good Parmesan cheese.

It was during one of our myriad pasta dinners that Miranda introduced me to pesto, and over the years, I have made good use of her recipe, which substitutes walnuts for the usual pine nuts. Below is my most recent pesto brainstorm, a vegetable dish so wholeheartedly green, it can only be called Green Goddess—a fitting tribute to the young mothers we once were.

This recipe can be made with an array of green veggies—whatever is in season or looks nicest to you. If homemade pesto is out of reach, you might buy some ready-made in a jar; just read the ingredients—they should look fairly close to the recipe below. Make sure pesto is at room temperature before mixing it with the pasta. If preparing it specifically for this dish, just leave it on the counter until you're ready to use it.

PESTO
4 cloves garlic, peeled
40 large or 50 medium basil leaves
½ c. walnuts
1½ c. Parmigiano Reggiano, grated
½ c. extra virgin olive oil
¼ tsp. sea salt, or more to taste
Freshly ground black pepper to taste

Blend garlic and basil in food processor until minced fine. Add walnuts and blend again, stopping to scrape sides down once or twice with a rubber spatula. Add grated Parmesan and whir again until cheese is fully integrated and mixture looks like a thick, bright green paste. Scrape stubborn bits off the sides. Turn food processor back on, pouring extra virgin olive oil slowly through the spout until all ingredients are combined and pesto is the consistency of a thin paste. You might not need all of the oil. Stop the food processor before sauce gets runny; it should be just thick enough to completely coat the pasta and veggies. Add salt and pepper to taste. Use half of prepared pesto for this dish.

PASTA
1 lb. long pasta, cooked al dente
About 1 lb. fresh asparagus
2 - 3 Tbsp. extra virgin olive oil
2 - 3 Tbsp. butter
Sea salt and freshly ground black pepper to taste
1 c. fresh or frozen green peas
1 large or 2 small zucchini
½ Pesto recipe (previous page)
Freshly grated Parmesan for serving

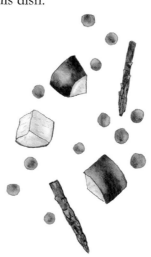

Set pot of water boiling for pasta, salting it to taste almost like the sea. Bend each stalk of asparagus from the thick end until it snaps, and discard it even if it is a third of the stalk. (Just think of that part as inedible, like a corn husk or the pit of a fruit.) Cut remaining stalks into 2-inch pieces. In a preheated heavy-bottom skillet, add 1 Tbsp. olive oil and 1 Tbsp. butter, heating briefly. Add asparagus, a good pinch of salt, and black pepper to taste. Pan-roast on medium-high until asparagus has brown pan marks but is still bright green. Test with a fork; it should be just tender but nowhere near mushy. Remove to a bowl.

While the pasta is cooking, cut zucchini into 1-inch cubes and repeat above steps for pan-roasting. Set aside with asparagus. Repeat again for peas—they require only a couple of minutes. Cover to keep warm.

Drain pasta and place in a shallow, wide bowl. Spoon about a quarter of pesto on top of hot pasta and toss with tongs until all strands are covered. Add pan-roasted veggies and another quarter of pesto, tossing again thoroughly but gently, until dish glows green throughout. Add more pesto as needed. Serve immediately, passing around freshly grated Parmesan. *Serves 4 to 8.*

PENNE ALLA VODKA

Penne alla Vodka is a relative newcomer to the culinary scene, and brings with it an ongoing debate as to its provenance: Some food historians say it was the invention of a New York chef named James Doty; others suggest the source of the recipe was the Dante restaurant in Bologna, Italy. The daughter of a chef named Luigi Franzese claims that her father, a native of Naples, created it at New York's Orsini Restaurant in the 1970s. And a fourth theory is that it was created by a chef who worked for a vodka company in 1980s Rome. The mystery of its origin is as intoxicating as the dish itself.

Wherever it began, this rich sauce is best made at the height of summer, when tomatoes are at their peak. If they are not in season, you could skip the blanching step (see below) and use a large can of diced or crushed Italian tomatoes instead. The sauce will be a little darker, but it will still be marvelous. I don't recommend substituting anything lowfat for the heavy cream, as it will change the sauce's texture—but if you must, half and half is the limit before things get really dire. This dish is best served right after mixing the sauce with the pasta. If you need to reheat, try adding a pat of butter and a drop of cream.

Penne alla Vodka is a simple recipe, but its effect is striking: the cream turns the tomatoes a gorgeous sunset color and neutralizes their acidity, softening the flavor—that is, until the vodka adds its own sharp, distinctive notes right back in.

3 large, ripe tomatoes, blanched (see below)
12 oz. penne, rigatoni, or any short pasta
1 Tbsp. extra virgin olive oil
3 Tbsp. butter, divided
1 medium onion, chopped small
3 cloves garlic, minced
Pinch of red pepper flakes
½ tsp. sea salt
¼ c. pasta water
¼ c. tomato paste
¼ c. vodka
½ c. heavy cream
½ c. grated Parmigiano Reggiano, plus more for serving

To blanch tomatoes, set a large pot of liberally-salted water to boil. When water is boiling, place a steamer basket or strainer in pot, add whole tomatoes, cover, and steam for 2 to 4 minutes until skins split. Remove carefully, running under cold water until cool enough to pull skins off. Chop skinned tomatoes on a rimmed board or plate so you don't lose any juice. Reserve tomato-tinged water to cook pasta just until al dente, starting it about halfway through making sauce.

Heat a skillet to medium high, adding olive oil and 1 Tbsp. butter. Add onions, turn heat down, and sauté until soft but not brown, about 10 minutes. Turn heat back up to medium-high and add chopped tomatoes with their juices, simmering until they begin to break down, about 5 minutes. (Start cooking pasta now.) Add garlic to skillet, turn heat down again, and cook until tomatoes are completely deconstructed, another 5 to 10 minutes. Use a potato masher or fork to smooth out any remaining lumps (it doesn't have to be perfect). Add salt, red pepper flakes, pasta water, and tomato paste, whisking until integrated into sauce.

Keeping tomato sauce at a high simmer, pour in vodka and cook until reduced by a third, about 3 minutes. Lower heat again until sauce is barely bubbling, and stir in ¼ c. Parmigiano Reggiano until melted. Add cream and stir until sauce turns pink, thick, and velvety. Drain pasta and add to skillet along with other ¼ c. Parmesan cheese, stirring until well coated. Serve immediately with more cheese on top, if desired. Perfect with an All-Green Salad. *Serves 3 to 5.*

CHEESE AND TOMATO VIDALIA PIE

Unlike the popular tomato cheese pies of the American South (apparently made with mayonnaise and cheddar), this pie leans heavily Italian with some French influences—a sort of cross between a quiche and a pizza. This dish was originally inspired by a recipe in Anna Thomas's *Vegetarian Epicure, Book Two*.

The Vidalia onion also has its roots in the American South. It was named after the town in Georgia where it first grew in the 1930s. I have heard people down south speak of Vidalias in tones bordering on reverence, and I can see why. They are exceptionally sweet due to the low amount of sulfur in the Georgia soil, and with their relatively short growing season, they have a rarefied air about them. I discovered Vidalia onions while living in Atlanta—David was doing his medical residency and I was mostly having babies. In those days, there was quite enough crying going on in our house already, and I was happy to find that I could chop these sweet onions without bringing on any more waterworks. I have been a fan of them ever since, not only because they never make me cry, but because they caramelize so nicely.

In this recipe, Vidalias are cooked until buttery and golden, laid over a bed of Parmigiano in a pie crust, and blanketed with a layer of fresh-cooked tomatoes. Whole milk mozzarella, more Parmigiano, and basil are layered in, and it's baked to perfection. This is a great company dish—it looks as gorgeous as it tastes.

SIMPLE PIE CRUST
1 c. unbleached all-purpose flour*
¼ tsp. salt
4 Tbsp. cold butter, cut into small chunks
3 Tbsp. cold water

*For a more nutritious crust, substitute up to two-thirds whole wheat flour; add up to 1 Tbsp. extra water. Preheat oven to 375 degrees and set aside a pie pan. In a bowl, combine flour and salt. Add chunks of butter, and work with your hands to thoroughly integrate until mixture looks like damp dirt. Gradually add cold water just until dough holds together but is not sticky; it will change consistency quickly as it comes together. Form dough into a ball, place on a floured surface, and use a rolling pin (or wine bottle) to roll it out into a circle just larger than your pie pan. Gently lift circle and lay it over the pan, pressing downward so the crust settles on the bottom. Crimp dough around edge of pan and trim excess with a knife. Poke a few fork holes in crust and prebake for 20 minutes. Remove and set aside, leaving oven on.

PIE FILLINGS

1 c. Parmigiano Reggiano, grated and divided
2 Tbsp. butter
3 - 4 Tbsp. extra virgin olive oil, divided
2 lb. Vidalia or other sweet onions
¾ tsp. salt
3 lb. ripe tomatoes (4 to 6 large), diced
2 cloves garlic, minced
Handful fresh basil, plus 6 whole leaves
½ lb. fresh whole milk mozzarella
Freshly ground black pepper to taste
Kalamata olives, optional

VIDALIA FILLING

Grate cheese and set aside. Heat a large, heavy-bottomed skillet, add butter and one Tbsp. olive oil and let them liquefy. Slice onions thinly and add to skillet with ¼ tsp. salt, cooking at medium-high until they become translucent and start to render their sugars. Turn heat down and continue cooking, stirring occasionally, until onions are very soft, golden brown, and greatly reduced in volume, about 30 minutes. Sprinkle half of Parmesan into prebaked pie shell and spread caramelized onions on top in an even layer.

TOMATO FILLING (RED SAUCE)

Add remainder of olive oil to skillet, turn heat to medium-high, and add chopped tomatoes and minced garlic. Set aside 6 basil leaves for top, and chiffonade remainder of basil (roll up tightly and slice into ribbons), adding to pan. Cook until tomatoes begin to break down, then turn heat to medium low and add ½ tsp. salt and black pepper to taste. Continue cooking until mixture is reduced by half, liquid is mostly gone, and a thick sauce has formed, about 20 minutes.

Spread tomato filling over onions. Cut fresh mozzarella into rounds and set on top, sprinkling with remainder of Parmesan. Arrange reserved basil leaves in a flower in the center, with olives in between if desired, brushing a little oil on basil leaves. Bake for 35 to 40 minutes, until cheese is browning and tomatoes are bubbling. Remove from oven and allow to set for 5 to 10 minutes before serving. Fabulous hot or at room temperature, paired with Florentine Fennel and Cabbage Salad. *Serves 3 to 5.*

APRICOT CHUTNEY-GLAZED SALMON

Atlantic salmon is found in many regions of the northern hemisphere, including the coast of Connecticut, where I spent my later childhood and where I'm living again as I finish writing this cookbook. The Connecticut shoreline is the southernmost tip of salmon's North American route, which extends all the way to Arctic Canada and northern Labrador. They most often hatch in fresh water, migrate to the ocean, and then come back to fresh water to reproduce; legend has it that they return to exactly the same place where they first hatched. This is not unequivocally proven, but it certainly makes a case for the natural instinct to return to whatever feels like home.

Chutney is a type of condiment that originates in India, traditionally made of fruits or vegetables cooked with vinegar, sugar, and spices. It's a cross between a relish and a jam, but with its own distinct and intense character. In this case, that intensity of flavor comes from cinnamon and apricot, garlic and ginger. I am always thinking up new ways to use apricots, for which I have an abiding fondness (see also Apricot Mandelbrot), and this recipe calls for dried California apricots, which are halved and sun-dried, with a brighter color and a much more intense flavor than the whole Turkish or Mediterranean variety. To me, they are like little bundles of sun.

I have served this chutney with chicken (see Almond-Crusted Chicken with Apricot Dipping Sauce), and have spread it on a round of brie wrapped in puff pastry and baked it for a dynamite *brie en croûte*. But it was this pairing with salmon that became a fast favorite among friends and family. I must have made this dish a hundred times by now, and it never disappoints: the sweet, tangy glaze with just a touch of heat is a perfect complement to the mild, tender flesh of the salmon. It comes out a deep, burnt-orange color and presents beautifully at the table. *Serves 4 to 6.*

BROILED SALMON
1½ - 2 lbs. salmon fillet, rinsed
¼ tsp. salt
Freshly ground black pepper

Place salmon in broiler pan or foil-lined baking dish and sprinkle with salt and pepper. Set aside on counter.

APRICOT CHUTNEY
1 c. apricot nectar, or apricot jam or fruit spread
2 Tbsp. soy sauce
2 Tbsp. agave or honey (omit if using jam/fruit spread)
2 to 4 Tbsp. water (omit if using nectar)
1 tsp. cinnamon
1 Tbsp. fresh grated ginger, or ½ tsp. dried
2 cloves minced garlic
Pinch of cayenne pepper
1 c. dried California apricots, snipped

Place all ingredients except apricots in saucepan over medium heat, whisking together. Since apricot nectar is not easy to find everywhere, apricot jam or fruit spread can be used instead, adding ¼ c. hot water and omitting agave or honey. (Do not use sugar-free jam.) Snip dried apricots into small pieces with scissors and add. Bring to a boil, lower to simmer, and cook until thickened and reduced by about one-third, about 20 to 30 minutes. Stir occasionally to prevent chutney from burning. When done, it should be sticky and both sweet and tart, with enough salt for contrast, and a tiny kick. Taste and adjust as needed. Keep warm.

When chutney is well reduced, preheat broiler on high. Place salmon under broiler, close to heat, and broil for 8 to 12 minutes, depending on thickness of fillet. When sides and top of fish are pale pink but center is still orange, remove from oven and spoon about a third of chutney on top, spreading with a pastry brush to coat evenly. Return to oven and set a timer for just 90 seconds, removing again promptly so sugars in chutney don't burn. Salmon should be pale pink most of the way through but not fully; it will continue cooking out of the oven. Tent with foil until ready to serve. Pass around remaining warm chutney at the table. Spectacular with Mixed Roasted Potato Wedges and Haricots Verts with Toasted Onions.

AGAVE LIME SALMON WITH HONEYDEW SALSA

This delicious salmon preparation pairs the robust tones of salsa with sweet, floral honeydew. Salsa has its origins in the Mesoamerican and Andean cultures, and honeydew has been cultivated for centuries in the Middle East, though its provenance can't be confirmed. You might find it odd to think of mixing fruit with garlic and cayenne pepper, but they flow together beautifully, as in my Apricot Chutney recipe (see previous page). If you can't find honeydew, any other ripe melon will work as well. The flavors of this melon salsa only need a short time to marry before it can be served over the citrusy broiled salmon. Though you can eat it all year round, this is a light, summery dish, humming with flavor and so pretty!

Prepare the salsa first, letting it sit on the counter for at least a half-hour and up to 3 hours before serving, and giving it a gentle stir every so often.

HONEYDEW SALSA
½ ripe honeydew, seeded, diced into ½-inch pieces
2 - 3 Persian cucumbers, or 1 European, diced small
1 whole sweet bell pepper, diced small
2 Tbsp. red onion, diced very fine
2 cloves garlic, minced
1 - 2 Tbsp. agave nectar
¼ c. olive oil
Juice of 2 good-sized limes
½ tsp. sea salt
Pinch cayenne pepper, or more to taste
Large handful cilantro, chopped fine

Dice melon, cucumbers, sweet pepper, and red onion as uniformly as possible in progressively smaller pieces, placing in a glass or ceramic (nonreactive) bowl. Add minced garlic, agave, olive oil, lime juice, salt, and cayenne, stirring and adjusting the sweet-spicy balance as needed: the goal is to taste both—a hint of sweetness, an echo of heat—without letting either one dominate. Add chopped cilantro and stir again gently. If serving more than 3 hours later, place in fridge until an hour before serving, then bring to room temperature and stir well before spooning over salmon. Leftovers keep for a day or two in the fridge.

AGAVE-LIME SALMON

1½ to 2 lbs. salmon fillet, rinsed and patted dry
Juice of 2 limes
1 tsp. ground cumin
¼ c. extra virgin olive oil
¼ tsp. salt, plus more for sprinkling
Freshly ground black pepper to taste
1 Tbsp. agave nectar

Place salmon in a baking dish or broiler pan and sprinkle with salt and pepper. Preheat broiler on high.

Juice the limes, and combine juice in a small bowl with olive oil, cumin, and ¼ tsp. salt, whisking together well. Brush lime mixture on salmon, repeating several times and making sure to cover whole surface. Pour any remaining mixture over fish. Do not add agave yet, or the sugar will burn under the broiler.

Broil salmon for 9 to 12 minutes, depending on thickness. Do not overcook. When fish is pale pink around the sides but not all the way to the center, it's done. (It will continue to cook for a couple of minutes after it is removed from oven.) Brush again with drippings and drizzle agave nectar over salmon immediately.

Serve with honeydew salsa, either spooned over fish or passed around. If keeping salsa on the side, re-brush fish with lime and olive oil mixture from pan just before serving to deepen the color. Wonderful with Famous Squash Pie, Creamed Cauliflower, or Duchess Potatoes. *Serves 4 to 6.*

Swiss-Style Lake Trout with Tiny Herbed Potatoes

The last time I returned to Switzerland in 2017, I could not get enough of the fresh lake trout that was offered on almost every menu, usually with buttery, herb-flecked potatoes. I just kept ordering it. Every time, it tasted as if the fish had jumped out of the water and straight into the chef's skillet—which might have been true, since I was almost always sitting in a lakefront restaurant. Switzerland's lakes are a wonder: deep teal blue and draped over the rolling landscape like swaths of fine silk.

This recipe is good with any white, flaky fish. I am particularly fond of lake trout (a kind of char), rainbow trout, barramundi, and branzino (Mediterranean sea bass). When I can't get fresh fish, I buy it flash-frozen which still tastes great. To quickly defrost, create a "bath" for the fish: Simply remove any outer packaging, leave the clear, inner shrink-wrap in place, and put in a large bowl of cool water in the sink. Keep the faucet trickling into the bowl, so the bath remains warmer than the fish. It should be ready to cook in about 15 minutes.

The herbed potatoes in those Swiss lakeside restaurants are usually peeled and they are not always tiny. But I like to use the teeny yellow or red ones because their skins are so new and delicate that peeling them is redundant. If using larger potatoes, consider peeling before you quarter and boil them—but only if you have the time. The beauty of this dish is how fast it comes together and how impressive it tastes.

Tiny Herbed Potatoes

1 lb. tiny potatoes, yellow, red, or a mixture
Generous pinch sea salt
2 Tbsp. butter
½ to 1 tsp. onion salt, to taste
2 Tbsp. flat-leaf parsley, chopped, or 1 tsp. dried
Freshly ground black pepper to taste

Wash potatoes and place in a medium saucepan with enough water to cover. Add a good pinch of sea salt and cover. Bring to a boil, then turn down and simmer until potatoes are soft, about 15 to 20 minutes. While potatoes are boiling, cook fish. (We will come back to the potatoes.)

FISH
1½ to 2 lbs. lake trout, char, barramundi, or branzino fillets
Zest and juice of one lemon
2 Tbsp. butter, softened
Sea salt and freshly ground black pepper to taste

If fish was frozen, press any excess water out of fillets with a clean tea towel or paper towel, repeating on both sides. Sprinkle liberally with sea salt and freshly ground black pepper. Turn over and repeat.

Zest lemon, using a microplane (a tiny grater) if you have one, as it captures all of the zest without any of the bitter white pith. Place zest in a bowl with softened butter. Add a good pinch of salt and a grind or two of black pepper, and use a fork to mash seasoned butter with zest and seasonings, creating a lemon butter.

Preheat a heavy, nonstick skillet on high. Place two plates as close as safely possible to the hot burner, so they warm as you cook. Add about a third of lemon butter to skillet and turn heat down to medium-high. As butter begins to brown, add fish fillets, cooking for 2 to 3 minutes. Flip fillets over and add another third of lemon butter. Allow to cook for 2 more minutes, watching closely. When the fish has become completely opaque and is beginning to turn golden, add remainder of lemon butter just until melted.

Remove fish immediately to warm plate, using a rubber spatula to scrape out all the beautiful lemon butter and drizzle it on top. If you wish, squeeze more lemon juice from your zested lemon over the fish. Cover with second warm plate.

Now, back to the potatoes. When they can be easily pierced with a fork, drain and return to saucepan with heat turned low. Add butter, onion salt, parsley, and black pepper to taste, stirring to coat. Keep warm, covered, until ready to serve

Serve fish with potatoes, and maybe with a side plate of Florentine Shaved Fennel and Cabbage Salad. Voilà! Unbeatable dinner in under thirty minutes. *Serves 4 to 6.*

ROTINI WITH SALMON, FETA, AND TOMATOES

This one-dish dinner is bursting with Mediterranean flavors that are perfect complements to the salmon. Try to get a good quality feta cheese in a whole block that you can crumble by hand. Don't use fat free feta, as it will not taste the same and won't melt nicely. This dish has a pretty color palette, and the feta melts gloriously when the hot pasta hits it, turning creamy while still retaining its salty intensity. *Serves 3 to 5.*

12 oz. rotini (or other short pasta)
3 - 4 Tbsp. extra virgin olive oil
1 lb. salmon fillet, pref. skinless (*see below for skin-on)
Salt and freshly ground black pepper to taste
1 c. scallions, sliced (or one small red onion, chopped fine)
2 large, ripe tomatoes, chopped
2 cloves garlic, minced
Handful fresh basil, chiffonaded
½ c. pitted Kalamata olives, cut in half (optional)
4 oz. good feta cheese, full fat, crumbled by hand

Set a pot of liberally salted water to boil. Cook rotini until just al dente. Make sauce while pasta is cooking. Heat a large skillet on medium-high and add 2 Tbsp. olive oil. Cut skinless salmon into midsize chunks, sprinkle with salt and pepper, and add to skillet. Turn heat down to medium and cook, stirring often, until fish is pale pink—about 5 minutes. *For skin-on fillet, place skin-side down in hot oiled skillet, flipping after 3 or 4 minutes. Use a fork to loosen and remove skin. Break fish into chunks and cook until pale pink.

Remove salmon from skillet and set aside. Do not wipe out pan. Add remainder of olive oil, turn up heat to medium-high, add scallions or red onion and sauté until beginning to brown, 3 to 5 minutes. Add tomatoes and sauté briefly. Add garlic and basil and cook for 1 to 2 minutes more, just until garlic is fragrant but tomatoes have not broken down all the way. Add salmon back to skillet, stirring to rewarm and combine with sauce. Adjust salt and pepper to taste. Add olives last, or serve on the side.

Place half of feta in a shallow bowl. Add hot pasta, then salmon tomato mixture. Use rubber spatula to scrape flavorful oil from skillet. Toss pasta to coat. Sprinkle remaining feta over pasta and serve immediately.

SHABBAT ROAST CHICKEN WITH THYME ONION JAM

This is our go-to dish for Shabbat dinners, Passover Seders, celebrations, and even weeknights when we just need something really good to eat. I think kosher chickens are the best: they have been soaked and salted (brined) as part of their preparation, so they are always juicy and flavorful. This roast chicken is a simple, basic recipe, to which many other flavors can be added. Try it with smoked paprika, curry powder, or herbs, or slather with the Thyme Onion Jam below as soon as it comes out of the oven. *Serves 4 to 6.*

1 Kosher chicken, cut into eighths
½ tsp. garlic powder, or more to taste
½ tsp. sea salt, or more to taste
Freshly ground black pepper to taste

Preheat oven to 450 degrees. Rinse chicken and pat dry. Arrange pieces in a single layer in a large roasting pan. Sprinkle liberally with salt, pepper, and garlic powder. Roast for 50 to 60 minutes, until juices run clear and skin is crisp and browned. Spoon drippings over the chicken just before serving, so it glows.

THYME ONION JAM

2 - 3 Tbsp. extra virgin olive oil
6 large sweet onions (like Mayan or Vidalia), sliced thin
½ tsp. salt, or more to taste
¼ c. honey
1 bunch fresh thyme, stripped and chopped
1½ c. hot chicken broth

Preheat a large pot at medium-high and add olive oil to cover bottom. Add sliced onions and salt, sautéing until fragrant, about 5 minutes. Turn down to medium and cook, stirring often, and adding a little broth if onions stick, about 20 minutes. When soft, golden, and reduced by half, add thyme, honey, and remaining broth. Continue simmering until broth is absorbed, onions have melted, and mixture is thick and jammy, 15 to 20 more minutes. Spread on roast chicken or serve on the side. Marvelous with Curried Fruited Rice.

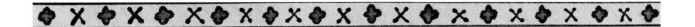

CHICKEN WITH ROASTED GARLIC, POTATOES, LEMON, AND TOMATOES

Garlic is one of the oldest cultivated plants in the world, mentioned in some of our first written historical records. It originated in central Asia, and the earliest known evidence of its existence—found in the Cave of the Treasure near Ein Gedi, Israel—dates back to around 4000 BCE. Fifteen hundred years later, it had spread throughout the Mediterranean, China, and India, prized not only for its flavor but for its medicinal and magical properties. Over the millennia, garlic has been credited with everything from warding off demons to curing respiratory ailments, and has been hailed as both an aphrodisiac and a fountain of youth.

Garlic belongs to the onion family, along with leeks, scallions, and shallots. The word "garlic" is derived from the Old English *gārlēac*, meaning "spear leek," due to the bulb's resemblance to a spearhead. When garlic is minced, combined with oil, and cooked at high heat, it releases an intense aroma and flavor that infuses everything it touches. But when garlic bulb is roasted whole inside its skin, it becomes a soft, mild paste that can be squeezed out and used as a spread. This recipe combines both in one glorious dish. I use fresh tomatoes when they are in season, but I have had good success with canned, diced tomatoes as well. If fresh basil is out of reach, use dried basil or try substituting Italian flat-leaf parsley. The bright flash of lemon juice is multiplied by the zest, adding high notes of contrast to the robustness of the garlic.

The key to this recipe is to use all of the salt and all of the oil. The potatoes will absorb every bit of seasoning you can throw at them, and all the vegetables need the coating of oil to brown instead of burning while they are waiting for the chicken to render its drippings. The smell when it's in the oven is enough to draw your whole household, one by one, into the kitchen to see what in the world…

4 large yellow potatoes, unpeeled, diced large
1 large or two small onions, diced large
3 large, ripe tomatoes, diced (or 28-oz. can diced)
4 cloves garlic, minced
1 tsp. dried rosemary
Handful chopped fresh basil (or 1 tsp. dried)
2 tsp. salt, divided, or more to taste
Freshly ground black pepper to taste
¼ c. extra virgin olive oil, plus more for rubbing on garlic cloves
2 lemons, zested and juiced
1 Kosher chicken cut in eighths, skin on
4 whole garlic bulbs

Preheat oven to 450 degrees. Place diced potatoes, onions, and tomatoes in a non-reactive bowl with minced garlic cloves, rosemary, chopped basil, several grinds of black pepper, and 1 tsp. salt. Add oil, half of lemon zest, and lemon juice, tossing well until evenly coated. Set aside.

Rinse and dry chicken. Sprinkle with remaining salt, pepper, and dried rosemary. Rub remaining lemon zest into chicken skin, distributing as well as possible.

Spread potato and tomato mixture in bottom of a very large roasting pan. Rub 4 whole garlic bulbs with a little olive oil and nestle in corners among vegetables. Arrange chicken on top of vegetables with as much space between pieces as possible. Potatoes, tomatoes, and garlic will catch the fat as it renders off the chicken and everything will cook at once. Do not crowd pan or potatoes will not brown.

Roast for one hour, checking with a fork to see if potatoes are soft, and checking chicken to be sure juices are running clear. Cook for an additional 15 minutes as needed, depending on doneness of potatoes and chicken. Be sure to spoon out drippings when serving, and encourage those at your table to taste the roasted whole garlic. Haricots Verts with Toasted Onions are a perfect accompaniment. *Serves 4 to 6.*

GARLIC LEMON CHICKEN BREASTS

I have used this recipe a thousand times with a hundred variations: it can be grilled or pan-fried, prepared with lime and cumin instead of lemon, cut up with pasta and veggies, as part of a salad, as part of a mixed grill platter, or as a main dish with sides—just to name a few. The key is always the same: don't overcook the chicken. If it's no longer pink inside, it's done! With a chicken tender or thin-pounded boneless chicken breast, this takes a *maximum* of 8 minutes. Beyond that, it can quickly become dry and unappetizing. A few easy tricks will ensure a perfect breast every time. Use a meat mallet to get a nice, evenly thin chicken breast by pounding gently between two pieces of plastic wrap (in a pinch, a large, flat-bottom mug or wine bottle will do). When cooking, use a timer as it always cooks faster than you expect. A dusting of flour (a European tradition) adds a distinct toastiness to the breast, though this isn't necessary, so those who are avoiding gluten can still make this dish. Done right, a chicken breast is a great delight, moist and tender enough to cut with a fork. Here are two ways to do it.

4 garlic cloves, minced
2 - 3 lemons at room temperature, zested, then halved and juiced
¼ c. extra virgin olive oil, plus extra if pan-frying
2 - 3 boneless, skinless chicken breasts, about ½ lb. each
Salt and freshly ground black pepper to taste
An additional lemon, cut into wedges, for serving
2 Tbsp. unbleached flour or cornstarch (dredging method only)

MARINADE AND GRILL METHOD

For marinade, combine minced garlic, lemon juice and zest, and olive oil in a large casserole dish. Cover chicken breasts with plastic wrap and gently pound to an even thickness (¼ to ½ inch thick). Nestle them into marinade, turning over to coat both sides. Marinate 30 to 60 minutes, turning chicken over with a fork occasionally. They are safe to remain at room temperature for that long and will cook more quickly. Don't marinade boneless breasts for longer than an hour, as the acid in the lemon will begin to break them down.

Preheat grill or grill pan, and discard marinade. Salt and pepper chicken on both sides. If using a grill, place chicken on hottest part and close lid; if using a grill pan, don't cover. Set a timer for 4 minutes; turn chicken over and cook 2 minutes more. Slice into largest piece to check that it is no longer pink; cook 1 to 2 more minutes if needed. Remove immediately from heat and platter, scattering lemon wedges over all.

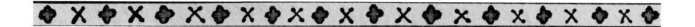

DREDGE AND PAN-FRY METHOD

Cover chicken breasts with plastic wrap and gently pound them to a uniform thickness, about ¼ to ½ inch. On a dinner plate, mix 2 Tbsp. flour, half of lemon zest, about ½ tsp. salt, and a few grinds of pepper. Dredge (drag) the flattened breasts through mixture on both sides to coat, shaking off firmly. Set aside in a single layer. (If making gluten free, try almond flour or a beaten egg instead.)

In a small bowl, mix chopped garlic with remainder of lemon zest and 2 Tbsp. olive oil so it forms a paste. Set bowl next to stove.

Preheat heavy-bottom skillet to medium-high. Add enough oil to cover bottom of skillet, at least 2 Tbsp. When oil is hot, place chicken breasts carefully in skillet. They should not overlap or touch. If you have a smaller skillet, you will almost certainly need to do this in two or more batches.

Allow breasts to brown for 2 minutes (use a timer), then squeeze half a lemon over the chicken in the pan (try squeezing the lemon into your hand, letting juice run through your fingers and catching seeds at the same time). Lemon has more sugar in it than you'd think, and it aids in caramelizing the chicken. Let brown for 2 more minutes, then turn over.

By now, the pan will be quite hot. Turn down to medium, and add more oil if needed (oil should be visible in pan). Set a timer for 2 minutes. Turn to bowl of lemon garlic paste and, using a rubber spatula or the back of a spoon, quickly spread paste on top of chicken. When 2 minutes are up, underside of chicken should be browning nicely. Turn over again briefly to cook lemon garlic paste and finish browning the other side, 1 to 2 minutes maximum. Make a small cut in largest piece to be sure inside is no longer pink, then remove chicken breasts to platter. Squeeze another half lemon over chicken. Tent with foil if making a second batch, remembering to add more oil to the pan (watch cooking time, as pan will be hotter to start with). When you've plated the last batch, cut a fresh lemon into wedges, and arrange on the plate for serving, if desired.

Either preparation is delicious with Curried Fruited Rice or Corn and Tomato Linguine; sliced on the bias and tossed with an All-Green Salad; or with Creamed Cauliflower and Pan-Roasted Asparagus with Garlic and Sea Salt. *Serves 2 to 4.*

ALMOND-CRUSTED CHICKEN WITH APRICOT DIPPING SAUCE

The apricot, with its evocative names like "the moon of faith," "the precocious one," and "the yellow plum," is a member of the rose family, and a cousin to the almond, the cherry, the peach, and the plum. It was cultivated in China and Central Asia as early as 2000 BCE, traveling by horseback in the saddlebags of nomadic traders via the Silk Road into Persia and Eurasia, and eventually proliferating into some seventy varieties in temperate climates around the world.

The vast majority of Switzerland's apricots grow in the Valais Valley, with the gorgeous red-orange Luizet as the most prized variety. I have loved apricots since I was a child, and I could talk about them all day (see Apricot Mandelbrot and Apricot-Chutney Glazed Salmon for starters). The poet John Ruskin describes them as "shining in a sweet brightness of golden velvet."

This dish, inspired by one of Susie Fishbein's *Kosher by Design* recipes, became an instant family favorite one Passover, when I had the idea of coating chicken tenders with ground almonds to recreate the toasty, crunchy flavor of schnitzel without the "forbidden" bread crumbs. This dish is wonderful for parties and for young kids; unlike many other Passover favorites, this one trailed us happily through the rest of our year, loved for its contrast of sweet and heat, its finger-foodliness, and the fun of individual dipping bowls. The apricot dipping sauce can easily be made in advance; either way, I recommend making it first.

APRICOT CHUTNEY DIPPING SAUCE

1 c. apricot nectar, or apricot jam or fruit spread
2 Tbsp. soy sauce
2 Tbsp. agave or honey
1 tsp. cinnamon
1 Tbsp. fresh grated ginger, or ½ tsp. dried
2 cloves garlic, minced
Pinch of cayenne pepper
1 c. dried California apricots, snipped
Up to ¼ c. hot chicken broth

Place all ingredients except dried apricots and chicken broth in a saucepan, whisking together in order given. If using jam instead of nectar, add ¼ c. hot water and omit agave or honey. Snip apricots into small pieces with scissors and add to saucepan. Bring mixture to a boil, then lower to simmer and cook until thickened and reduced by about one-third, usually about 20 to 30 min. Stir occasionally to be sure sauce doesn't burn. Taste to adjust for sweet and savory balance. Once chutney has reduced and is thick and sticky, heat chicken broth in microwave. Add hot broth, 1 Tbsp. at a time, whisking until sauce is thin enough to dip chicken strips into.

ALMOND-CRUSTED CHICKEN
2 lb. boneless, skinless chicken breasts, pounded
½ c. honey
½ c. coarsely ground almonds (skins on)
½ tsp. paprika
2 tsp. garlic powder
¼ tsp. salt and freshly ground black pepper to taste

Preheat oven to 400 degrees. Lightly oil two cookie sheets.

Cover chicken breasts with plastic wrap and, using a meat mallet (or flat-bottom wine bottle), gently pound them to an even thickness of ¼ to ½ inch, then cut into strips on the bias, about 2 inches wide and 3 inches long. Place honey in a shallow bowl. On a dinner plate, mix ground almonds with paprika, garlic powder, salt, and pepper. Dip the chicken cutlet strips in honey, letting it drip off, then dredge strips in the almond mixture, placing them in a single layer on the cookie sheet as you go. Brush tops of strips with olive oil. Bake for 12 to 15 minutes, turning chicken over with tongs after 6 minutes or so and quickly brushing with oil again to brown evenly on both sides. Cut largest piece open to be sure insides are no longer pink, remove from oven, and use tongs to pile them on a platter to serve immediately.

This dish is perfectly complemented by Cara Cara Orange Salad with Cranberries and Caramelized Onions, or for a finger-food feast, alongside Mixed Roasted Potato Wedges and Pan-Roasted Asparagus with Garlic and Sea Salt. And if you're feeling extra-ambitious, may I suggest individual dishes of Sublime Chocolate Mousse for dessert, maybe even garnished with Mousse Meringues? *Serves 4 to 8.*

BARBECUE TURKEY MEATLOAF

This simple, homey dish has been shaped by the arc of American history. It begins with the native turkey, which has been part of Indigenous culture for many hundreds of years. Scholars have traced wild turkey to the cuisines of Mohawk, Onondaga, Huron, Ojibwe, and Shawnee tribes, among others.

Barbecue sauce is thought to have come from seventeenth century American colonies, but its provenance can't be verified. What is clear is that the earliest versions consisted of only vinegar, salt, and pepper. The 1920s saw the addition of sugar, Worcestershire sauce, and ketchup; and after World War II, the amount of sugar increased dramatically. I love the triangle of contrasts between the sweetness and sourness of barbecue and the savory richness of meat (for more sweet-and-sour dishes, see also Old World Stuffed Cabbage and Inside-Out Stuffed Cabbage).

The first meatloaf seems to have appeared in the United States in the 1870s as a breakfast recipe for using up leftover meat. It rose to great popularity as a dinner food in the 1940s, when the deprivations of war forced households to stretch hard-to-get ingredients like meat with cheaper, readily available starches. The traditional meatloaf used a combination of ground beef and pork mixed with eggs and milk-soaked bread.

In a kosher household, neither the pork nor any recipe that mixes meat with milk is permitted, so meatloaf was not in my repertoire as a young cook until I devised substitutes: I found a flavorful way to add moisture without milk using a slurry of eggs and onions, and replaced the beef and pork with ground turkey to lighten the dish. Swapping rolled oats for the bread makes it even lighter and more nutritious. The quick homemade barbecue sauce requires no precooking—it simply gets brushed on the meatloaf— and the result is super moist and light, blending summer barbecue with winter comfort food in a most appealing way. *Serves 6 to 8.*

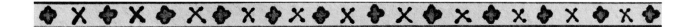

QUICK BBQ SAUCE
1 c. ketchup (I prefer Heinz™)
2 - 4 Tbsp. Worcestershire sauce
1 Tbsp. mustard
1 Tbsp. liquid smoke
Pinch cayenne pepper, or more to taste
3 Tbsp. dark brown sugar, or more to taste
¼ tsp. salt
Freshly ground black pepper to taste

Measure ketchup into a small bowl. Shake on Worcestershire sauce until it covers the surface of the ketchup. Whisk together. Add remaining ingredients and whisk again to combine all thoroughly. Taste to adjust seasonings. No need to cook—it will roast in the oven for well over an hour with the meatloaf.

TURKEY MEATLOAF
1 lb. ground turkey, pref. pasture-raised
1 lb. ground white meat turkey, pref. pasture-raised
½ c. rolled oats (not instant)
2 eggs
1 large onion, cut in eighths
1 generous tsp. salt
Freshly ground black pepper to taste

Preheat oven to 400 degrees. Mix both types of ground turkey in a bowl with rolled oats. Set aside. Place eggs, onion, salt, and pepper in a food processor, and whir until onions have blended into eggs. Add egg mixture to meat mixture and combine thoroughly (it will be very soft).

Spread meatloaf mixture evenly into a 9 x 13-inch baking dish and brush gently with Quick BBQ sauce. Cover with foil and place in center of oven for 45 minutes. Turn oven down to 350 degrees. Remove foil and brush top of meatloaf with BBQ sauce again. Bake uncovered meatloaf for another 30 minutes. Remove from oven and let sit for 5 minutes before serving. Keeps well in fridge for several days, or in freezer for up to 3 months. Absolutely delicious with Creamed Cauliflower and an All-Green Salad.

PAN-ROASTED DUCK BREAST WITH CLASSIC ORANGE SAUCE

Duck is a wonderful source of protein, but it's not very popular in America. Most restaurant dishes I've tried here, including classics like Peking Duck and Duck à l'Orange, tend to be heavy and oily. But as I learned recently at a tiny sidewalk restaurant in Cologne, Germany, duck breast can be tender, juicy, and light, like a cross between lean beef and dark meat chicken, with just the right touch of richness.

How did they do it? It turns out that making duck breast is not complex (and is a lot less costly than I imagined). It's true that duck is a high-fat fowl, but almost all of that fat is concentrated in the skin. If the skin is heated directly, the fat can be rendered (a culinary term for "collected"), leaving a breast that's moist and richly-flavored without being heavy. That's not to say it's quick, but this dish requires more patience than skill. I found that if I followed certain steps with care, it worked like a charm.

This recipe takes a solid hour to prepare, plus another 45 minutes beforehand to bring the duck breasts to room temperature before they're cooked—this is crucial for the success of the recipe. So plan ahead! You will also need a heavy-bottom sauté pan and a reliable meat thermometer.

PAN-ROASTED DUCK BREAST
1 lb. duck breasts, about 4 oz. each
Sea salt and freshly ground black pepper

1. Bring duck breasts to room temperature before cooking. Cooking them cold will cause them to seize up.

2. Place duck on a cutting board with the white (skin) side facing up. With a sharp knife, gently score skin in a tight crosshatch pattern, keeping scores about an eighth-inch apart. The more deeply you score, the less fat will be left on the breast, so work according to your tastes—but take care not to expose the flesh.

3. Season duck with salt, heavily on the skin side and lightly on the flesh side. Add black pepper to taste.

4. **Do not preheat your skillet!** Place duck breasts skin side down in unheated, heavy-bottom sauté pan. Now turn burner on to medium-low.

5. After about 5 minutes, the fat should begin to bubble gently. Maintain this gentle bubbling throughout cooking (about 20 to 30 minutes). If it is either silent or spitting loudly, adjust heat up or down accordingly. This will be more difficult with an electric stove than a gas flame; just do your best to stay ahead of it.

6. Every 7 to 10 minutes, pour off duck fat using the following method: Press down on duck breasts with a lid to stop them from falling out. Tip the skillet, moving slowly and with care, and pour fat into a heatproof bowl or cup. Continue cooking and pouring off fat every so often, until majority of fat layer has disappeared and skin is golden brown. Reserve duck fat for use in Classic Orange Sauce.

7. Check temperature of breast by piercing center with a meat thermometer until it reaches 125 degrees. Increase heat to medium-high, browning skin more if not yet golden brown, about 1 minute. Flip breast to cook meat side. You should only need 1 to 2 minutes for a medium rare breast. Pierce center of biggest piece with a meat thermometer to see when it registers 130 degrees. For medium, continue to 140 degrees. I don't recommend cooking beyond that, as it can dry out. Remove duck from pan and cover to keep warm. Without washing skillet out, use it to make sauce.

CLASSIC ORANGE SAUCE
½ c. dry white wine
1½ c. chicken stock
2 Tbsp. reserved duck fat (see above)
¼ c. fresh-squeezed orange juice
1 tsp. freshly grated orange zest
1 Tbsp. honey (optional)
Sea salt and freshly ground black pepper to taste

Place skillet over high heat. Deglaze with white wine (pour liquid into hot pan to release all the brown bits). Stir and turn heat down to medium-high, reducing wine until 1 or 2 Tbsp. remains, about 2 to 3 minutes. Add chicken stock, 2 Tbsp. rendered duck fat, orange juice and zest, plus honey, if using (recommended unless orange juice is very sweet). Reduce liquid again until sauce is sticky and dark, about 10 or 15 minutes. (If sauce is not thickening properly, dissolve 1 Tbsp. cornstarch in 2 Tbsp. cold chicken stock and pour in, whisking constantly until sauce thickens.) Remove from heat and season with salt and pepper to taste. Serve warm, passing sauce around in a gravy boat to pour over duck breasts. Marvelous with Curried Fruited Rice, an All-Green Salad, and Whole Berry Cranberry Sauce. *Serves 3 to 5.*

DRUNKEN ROAST BEEF WITH HERB AND OLIVE OIL RUB

Roast beef is a signature dish of England, with its deep roots expressed by the 1731 patriotic ballad, "The Roast Beef of Old England." In fact, this dish is so emblematic of British cooking that the French have nicknamed the Brits, *les rosbifs*. In 2015, my youngest son, Jesse, and I had the chance to sample roast beef at its source, when we found ourselves overseas at the same time and got to explore London together.

These days, I eat a lot less beef, given the implications of red meat production for our planet. I reserve roast beef for special occasions, and then I try to make sure it's grass-fed and even local, if possible. I view the roast as part of the celebration budget and buy the best cut of meat I can find. My favorite is a rib roast, beautifully marbled with fat so it remains moist throughout cooking. In this recipe, the meat is further enhanced by the double step of marinating in herbs and red wine first, then adding a second herb rub before roasting. The scent wafting from the oven is intoxicating, and the flavor is absolutely divine.

MARINATED RIB ROAST

4 to 5 lb. rib roast, pref. grass-fed
½ bottle good red wine
¼ c. soy sauce or tamari
4 cloves garlic, minced
½ c. extra virgin olive oil
¼ c. balsamic vinegar
1 tsp. dried rosemary
1 tsp. dried thyme
½ tsp. salt and freshly ground black pepper

You will need a roasting pan and a meat thermometer for this recipe.

Place rib roast in a large, sealable bag and place bag in a large baking pan (in case it leaks). Add all marinade ingredients to bag with the roast. Seal slowly, pushing out air, and turn over several times to mix. Marinate for at least 1 hour and up to 4 hours. Set a timer to turn bag over periodically.

Rib roast **must** be at room temperature when you put it in the oven, so refrigerate during marinating **only** if you are waiting more than 90 minutes to cook (then remove from fridge at least 1 hour before cooking).

Preheat oven to 425 degrees. Pour marinade from bag into a saucepan, setting aside to make gravy (perfectly safe as long as it's boiled thoroughly). Place beef in a roasting pan and slather with herb and olive oil rub.

HERB AND OLIVE OIL RUB

2 cloves garlic, minced
1 tsp. each: dried rosemary, sage, and thyme
2 Tbsp. extra virgin olive oil
1 tsp. sea salt and freshly ground black pepper to taste

Mix all ingredients into a paste and rub all over entire roast. Push meat thermometer deep into thickest part of meat. Place pan in center of oven and roast, uncovered, for about 1 hour, setting timer for 50 minutes and checking internal temperature of roast every few minutes from then on. For rare, meat should reach 135 to 140 degrees; for medium rare, 145 to 150 degrees; for medium, 155 to 160 degrees. When desired temperature is reached, remove immediately from oven and use a baster to siphon off drippings, adding to marinade in saucepan for gravy. Cover roast with foil to keep warm.

GRAVY

Reserved contents of marinade bag
Drippings from roasting beef
2 Tbsp. cornstarch
2 Tbsp. cold water
Salt and freshly ground black pepper

Bring drippings and marinade in saucepan to a rolling boil. Keep boiling for 5 minutes, watching carefully so it doesn't bubble over. Whisk cornstarch and cold water together in a small bowl to create a slurry. After liquid has boiled for full 5 minutes, turn down to simmer and pour in slurry, whisking constantly as liquid thickens. Add salt and pepper to taste. Keep warm until ready to serve, and don't forget to pass it around! Transfer roast to a rimmed cutting board and carve at the table so it doesn't get cold. Perfect with Mixed Roasted Potato Wedges, Cremini Mushrooms, and an All-Green Salad. I also recommend a hearty red wine like a Cabernet Sauvignon, or a Sorai or Valpolicella from the Veneto region of Italy. *Serves 8 to 12.*

ENTRÉES   89

RIB EYE STEAK CHIMICHURRI

Chimichurri is a versatile herb-and-garlic condiment that most likely has its origins with the *gauchos* of Argentina and Uruguay, skilled horsemen who spent their lives on the *pampas* range and often roasted their meat over open fires. The provenance of the name *chimichurri* is more uncertain: various theories connect it to the Basque word *tximitxuri,* meaning "hodgepodge," or the Spanish word *chirriburri,* meaning "hubbub." There is even a myth, never proven, that it is actually derived from the English words, *Jimmy's curry,* with Jimmy as the mispronounced name of a meat trader who was visiting Argentina.

My own experience with chimichurri is a lot less colorful: I learned to make it from watching celebrity chef Bobby Flay, who knows how to make use of the intense flavors of the Americas. The original chimichurri sauce combined herbs with oil and vinegar to create a bright green, super-flavorful paste, but Chef Bobby recommends using limes instead of vinegar, and the effect is marvelous.

I suggest a rib eye steak here, because I think it's the juiciest and most flavorful cut. If that's not available, ask the guy behind the meat counter to recommend something comparable—and try to make it grass-fed, if possible.

This recipe contains my personal favorite balance of flavors. Once you discover the magic of chimichurri—the contrast of the acid and fresh herbs with the richness of the meat—I hope you start experimenting, and come up with the balance of flavors that taste best to you. The only fixed points are garlic, flat-leaf parsley, and olive oil. Beyond that, whichever herb-and-acid mixture you like best is the right one.

CHIMICHURRI SAUCE
Large handful flat-leaf parsley
Large handful fresh basil
Large handful fresh cilantro
3 cloves garlic
Juice of 2 limes
¼ c. extra virgin olive oil
Sea salt
Freshly ground black pepper

Place all fresh herbs and peeled garlic cloves in food processor. Pulse several times until finely chopped and blended. Add lime juice and pulse again until a paste forms. With food processor on, pour olive oil slowly through spout until mixture becomes creamy and emulsified. Add a good pinch of salt and a few turns of black pepper, and pulse again until combined. Taste and adjust seasonings. Keeps well in the fridge for several days or can be frozen in ice cube trays for future use.

RIB EYE STEAK
4 boneless rib eye steaks, 10 - 12 oz. each
Salt and freshly ground black pepper to taste
Chimichurri sauce (above)

Set broiler on high or turn grill to medium-high. Sprinkle steaks generously with salt and pepper, and brush with a layer of chimichurri sauce before cooking, allowing them to sit during preheating. Broil or grill the steaks for about 4 minutes per side, depending on the thickness of the steaks and your desired level of doneness. This timing should yield medium-rare steaks; if you like them rare, cook 1 or 2 minutes less; for medium steaks, cook 2 or 3 minutes more. I don't recommend cooking beyond medium, as they lose all of their juiciness and distinct flavor. Remove from heat and let steaks sit for a minute or two before serving. Brush with more chimichurri sauce and pass around remainder in a small bowl at the table.

This dish is perfect alongside Cremini Mushrooms or Pan-Roasted Asparagus with Garlic and Sea Salt, and an All-Green Salad. Since steak is so rich, I like to serve it without a heavier side—but any potato dish would go well, too. And don't forget a hearty red wine! *Serves 4 to 6.*

OLD WORLD STUFFED CABBAGE

According to historians, stuffed cabbage rolls have been part of Jewish culinary traditions for as long as two thousand years. Numerous countries and cultures have laid claim to the dish—with a range of savory and sweet flavors—including Persia, Poland, Ukraine, Russia, and Germany, among others. I first tasted sweet-and-sour stuffed cabbage at the Second Avenue Deli in New York when I was eighteen and visiting the family of my college roommate and still dear friend, Alise. Her father, Arnie Young, was the most generous man I'd ever met; when he heard I had never been to this iconic deli before, he literally ordered everything on the menu. Every dish I tasted was delicious, but the stuffed cabbage felt like home.

So, this dish was one of the first I developed when I had my own kitchen. Thirty-five years later, it is an enduring family favorite, a dish I make every year for the holiday of Sukkot. This is the eight-day fall festival when we eat outside in a makeshift hut called a *sukkah*, both as a reminder of the forty years Jews spent wandering in the desert, and as an homage to the temporary dwellings of field workers during harvest-time. Sukkot reconnects us physically and emotionally with the land. Every year when the kids were small, we would build a *sukkah* in our yard and help them to adorn it with gourds, dried flowers, fairy lights, and their latest works of art. Then we would invite friends and family to come and share the magic. These days, we are not often together in our *sukkahs*, but whenever we feel that first chill of autumn, a steaming dish of stuffed cabbage is just right, no matter where we all are. With that first bite—the dark-and-light green of the cabbage together with the hearty beef and rice filling and the tangy sweet-and-sour sauce dotted with raisins—comes a rush of happy memories, warming us from the inside out.

This is a time-consuming recipe. Leave yourself 90 minutes to 2 hours for prep and assembly, and another hour to bake. (If you want the flavors of this dish but just don't have the time, see Inside-Out Stuffed Cabbage, next.) This recipe makes two large pans of stuffed cabbage (10 to 12 rolls each); they freeze well.

STUFFED CABBAGE ELEMENTS
2 heads steamed green cabbage for wrappers
6 c. cooked basmati rice, divided
Meat filling
Sweet-and-sour tomato sauce

Ingredients and directions follow for each element.

CABBAGE WRAPPERS

Place 2 whole cabbages in a large pot, add 6 cups water (about 3 inches), and bring to a boil. Turn down to an active simmer and steam, covered, until outer leaves turn dark green and cabbage can be pierced most of the way through with a fork, 35 to 50 minutes, depending on size. (While cabbage is steaming, make rice, below.) When done, cabbage should be tender but not falling apart. Remove carefully and allow to cool at least 30 minutes while assembling other components of the dish (meat filling and tomato sauce).

When cabbage is safe to handle, make a deep, cone-shaped cut around the base of each head and remove stem of cabbage. Slowly peel leaves apart, trying not to tear them (some tearing will occur; don't discard unless shredded). It will become more difficult to separate leaves as you go deeper—you might need to cut base back again. Do not use uncooked or tiny leaves. Stack on a dish towel in preparation for stuffing, with larger ones on top. You need 20 to 24 usable cabbage wrappers (aim for a couple of extra leaves).

BASMATI RICE

6 c. water
3 c. basmati rice
1 tsp. salt

In a saucepan, bring water, rice, and salt to a boil, then turn down. Simmer, covered, for 20 minutes, until water is absorbed. Remove cover and cool. This is enough rice for the filling and as a bed for serving stuffed cabbage: measure out 2 c. cooked rice for filling, then cover remainder and set aside.

MEAT FILLING

2 lbs. lean ground beef (or ground dark turkey)
2 c. cooked rice
2 large eggs
1 medium onion, quartered
1 generous tsp. salt
Freshly ground black pepper

Combine ground beef and cooked, cooled rice in a large bowl. In a food processor, combine eggs, salt, and onion, and pulse into a slurry. Pour onion mixture into beef mixture, season with black pepper, and mix with hands until thoroughly combined. Set filling aside while making sweet-and-sour tomato sauce.

SWEET-AND-SOUR TOMATO SAUCE

1 medium onion, quartered
2 28-oz cans plain crushed tomatoes
½ c. brown sugar, or more to taste
1 c. golden raisins, or more to taste
1 tsp. salt, or more to taste
Freshly ground black pepper to taste

Place quartered onion in food processor and whir until crushed. Pour into a large bowl with canned tomatoes, brown sugar, raisins, salt, and pepper, stirring well to mix. The sauce is the trickiest part, so be sure to taste it more than once before assembling the dish. The proportions are not completely fixed—some cans of tomatoes are sweeter than others, the onions might be more or less sharp, or the sauce might just taste different than you expect—so here is the balance you're aiming for: you can taste the sweetness of the brown sugar, but it is not cloying; the acidity of tomatoes and sharpness of onion should offset this sweetness. The salt should act as a foil for both sweet and sharp. Taste after adding brown sugar, and taste again after adding salt. The flavor of the raisins won't come out until they cook, when they will plump up gorgeously—the buried treasure in the dish.

STUFFED CABBAGE ASSEMBLY

Clear counter of everything but the bowl of sweet-and-sour sauce, bowl of meat filling, 2 large (9 x 13 in.) baking dishes, and cabbage wrappers. Use large cutting board or stretch of clean counter to stuff cabbage.

Place piles of cabbage leaves above cutting board (twelve o'clock) where you can reach them easily. They might still drip, so stack them on a clean cloth or paper towel. Put the bowl of beef filling on your left (9 o'clock), and the baking dish on your right (3 o'clock). Put the second baking dish somewhere within reach. Add a thin layer of sweet-and-sour sauce to both baking dishes, just enough to cover, then set sauce aside. You won't need it again until you've filled a whole pan with stuffed cabbage.

Start with the biggest cabbage leaves. Take a leaf and put it in the center of your workspace with the curved edge (the part that was attached to the stem) closest to you and facing up like a little cup. Take a generous spoonful of meat filling—enough to fill the center of your cupped palm (use considerably less when the leaves are small). Place filling in the little cup of the cabbage leaf. If there is no cup shape, set filling in the leaf at the spot where the cup would be (around 6 o'clock).

Roll the cabbage leaf from the bottom, one to two rotations, until about the middle of the leaf. Fold the left and right sides of the leaf in towards the middle, tucking in as you continue rolling to the end, making a little package. It will resemble an egg roll and be about the same size. If a leaf is torn, try to fold it in such a way that it still encloses the filling. But don't worry if you have to discard a few leaves—it's inevitable.

Proper placement in the baking dish will help to hold the rolls together as they cook. Place first roll at short end of baking dish, all the way to the left or right. The goal is to fit 2 rolls end to end, with 5 to 6 rows of rolls down the length of the dish. Continue in this way, placing the rolls together gently but tightly, placing larger rolls next to smaller ones as needed so they fit without squishing. When first pan is full, pour half of the sweet-and-sour sauce over the rolls, being sure to get half of the raisins, which will have sunk to the bottom of the bowl. Nudge the rolls a bit so some of the sauce can run down between them. Cover tightly with foil.

When first pan is filled, preheat oven to 350 degrees. Continue rolling cabbages and position in second pan. Cover with remainder of sauce, nudging rolls to let the sauce run down between them. Cover tightly.

Pans will be very heavy and will likely drip in the oven. Hold with two hands and, if possible, set in middle of oven, side-by-side, on top of cookie sheets or pieces of foil to catch drips. (If oven racks are small and you need to place pans one above the other, set a timer for 30 minutes and switch them.) Bake, covered, for at least one hour, until sauce is bubbling hard. Lift edges of foil on both pans to check, and if it isn't bubbling merrily, cook 15 to 30 minutes more, as needed.

Remove from oven and allow to rest, covered, while you rewarm remaining rice, adding a bit of water to saucepan so it can steam itself. Serve two pieces stuffed cabbage over a bed of rice as a main dish, or one piece without the rice as an appetizer. Add a generous spoonful of sweet-and-sour sauce to each roll.

If preparing a day or two ahead, a pan of stuffed cabbage will need a lot of time to reheat, so plan accordingly. Remove pan from fridge at least 2 hours before serving. Warm in a 200-degree oven for 2 hours or a 350-degree oven for 30 to 45 minutes, checking that rolls are heated through before serving. Can also be frozen in any quantity, tightly covered, for up to three months.

Whew! That was a lot of effort. But it's beautiful, isn't it? And you'll know it was worth it as soon as you taste this sweet and savory, soul-satisfying dish. True comfort food, Old World style. *Serves 10 to 20.*

INSIDE-OUT STUFFED CABBAGE

This recipe came about one winter when I was craving the flavors of Old World Stuffed Cabbage (see previous recipe) but simply didn't have the time or energy to make it the traditional way. While this version might be less impressive, it does capture the satisfying essence of the dish—and only takes 45 minutes to make. Gabriella and Louis have also made a vegetarian version using beef substitute and were very happy with the result. This recipe is for a crowd but can be halved if you're feeding a smaller circus. *Serves 8 to 10.*

INSIDE-OUT STUFFED CABBAGE ELEMENTS

Sweet-and-sour tomato beef layer
4 c. cooked basmati rice
Cabbage and onion layer

Ingredients and directions follow for each of these elements.

SWEET-AND-SOUR TOMATO BEEF LAYER

1 Tbsp. extra virgin olive oil, more as needed
2 lb. ground beef (or ground dark turkey, or beef substitute)
12 oz. tomato paste (2 small cans)
1½ c. water, more as needed
¼ c. brown sugar, or more to taste
½ tsp. salt, or more to taste
Freshly ground black pepper to taste
1 c. yellow raisins

Preheat a large skillet. Add 1 Tbsp. oil and ground meat. Stir and cook until meat is beginning to brown and produce drippings, about 10 minutes. (If using meat substitute, add an extra Tbsp. oil and be sure it's hot before frying the crumbles, so they get a little crispy.) Add tomato paste and water, stirring vigorously to combine. Add ½ tsp of salt, several grinds of black pepper, and brown sugar, tasting to find a balance you like between sweet, sour, and savory. (For more on this flavor balance, see page 94.) Bring sauce to a boil, then turn down and simmer for about 10 minutes. Add yellow raisins and cook for 10 more minutes, adding some water if sauce reduces greatly; it should be a soupy, velvety sauce. Cover and keep warm.

RICE
2 c. basmati rice
4 c. water
½ tsp. salt

In a saucepan, bring water, rice, and salt to a boil, then turn down. Simmer, covered, for 20 minutes, until all water is absorbed. Make cabbage and onion layer as rice cooks; they should be done at the same time.

CABBAGE AND ONION LAYER
2 Tbsp. extra virgin olive oil, more as needed
2 large onions, sliced
1 medium green cabbage, sliced thin
½ tsp. salt, or more to taste
Freshly ground black pepper to taste

In a preheated, very large skillet or soup pot, heat 1 Tbsp. oil on medium high. Add sliced onions, half of salt, and some pepper, sizzling until fragrant, translucent, and beginning to brown, 3 to 5 minutes. Turn down to medium and allow onions to continue softening and caramelizing while you thinly slice cabbage.

Add sliced cabbage, 1 Tbsp. oil, remainder of salt, and more pepper to pot; stir fry for 5 to 10 minutes, until cabbage is somewhat tender but not mushy (firmer is better for reheating). Cover until ready to serve.

To serve, evenly spread sweet-and-sour tomato beef layer in a wide, shallow serving dish. Top with cabbage and onion layer. Keep rice separate, serving a bed of it on each plate and nestling the saucy mixture on top.

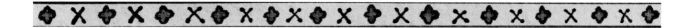

CREAMY VEGETABLE CURRY WITH GRAND FIXINGS

This is a wonderful dish for company because all the parts can be made in advance and reheated when you are ready to serve. The recipe itself is very flavorful and rich, and the "grand fixings" are a rainbow of toppings that add texture, freshness, and an element of fun, as each person at the table chooses their own.

Believe it or not, my love for curry originates in Switzerland, where mild curries are a staple of the cuisine. They were introduced to the Swiss in 1952 by Ueli Prager, the founder of the popular Mövenpick restaurants. He added an "exotic" new dish to the menu and called it *Riz Casmir,* a creamy curried chicken topped with various fruits and served on a bed of rice. It took off like wildfire, and by the time I was born in 1966, such curries were everywhere. My mother became very fond of them while living in Zurich, and made them often, so I grew up loving curry flavor—though I never developed a taste for the fiery, spicy kinds from Thailand, Vietnam, and the Indian subcontinent. The warm flavors of mild curry come from ground turmeric, coriander, cumin, ginger, red pepper, and any number of other spices. Basmati rice, with its lovely popcorn fragrance, is an important anchor for this dish. (For more on basmati rice, see page 112.)

In its basic form, this dish is vegan—a cross between a mild Indian *aloo gobi* and the Swiss cream curry I remember—with the fixings on a grand scale for contrast and fun. The toppings lend themselves to endless creativity; if you wish, you can add chicken or other protein as well (see below). The "grand fixings" do not go into the curry, but are placed in small, separate bowls in the center of the table, so each person can combine them as they wish. Offer whatever toppings appeal most to you, looking for a balance of savory, sweet, crunchy, and chewy to adorn this hearty and fragrant dish. *Makes about 6 to 10 servings.*

RICE
6 c. water
3 c. basmati rice
1 tsp. salt
1 tsp. olive oil

Bring water to a boil. Add rice, salt, and olive oil. Turn down and simmer, covered, until water is absorbed, 20 minutes. Set aside.

VEGETABLE CURRY

2 Tbsp. extra virgin olive oil
1 large onion, chopped
4 potatoes, peeled and cubed
2 tsp. mild curry powder, or more to taste
4 c. vegetable broth
1 cauliflower, cut into small, equal-sized pieces
3 pints cherry tomatoes, cut in half, or 3 tomatoes, chopped
1 bag (about 5 oz.) baby spinach
Large bunch fresh cilantro, chopped
1 Tbsp. honey, optional
1 tsp. salt and freshly ground black pepper to taste
1 c. coconut milk or coconut cream, or more to taste

While rice is cooking, preheat a large soup pot on medium-high and add olive oil, briefly letting it liquefy. Add chopped onions, turn heat to medium, and sweat for about 15 minutes until translucent and browning.

Add potatoes, 1 tsp. curry powder, and broth, turn heat to high, and bring to a boil. Turn down to simmer and allow potatoes to soften until they can be pierced with no resistance, about 15 minutes. Add cauliflower and tomatoes, cover, turn heat to low and let simmer for another 10 minutes. Add spinach and cilantro, remainder of curry, honey (if desired), salt and pepper, and stir. Pour in coconut milk or cream and stir again until evenly distributed, allowing to simmer for another few moments to combine flavors. Other creamy liquids can be substituted for the coconut, including dairy cream or soy or cashew milk. But I think the cool flavor of coconut complements the warmth of the curry beautifully.

In the breaks between steps for the curry, prepare protein, if desired, and grand fixings (see next page).

OPTIONAL PROTEIN

1 Tbsp. extra virgin olive oil
3 boneless chicken thighs or 6 veggie sausage patties, diced
½ tsp. mild curry powder
½ tsp. sea salt

Heat oil in preheated skillet. Add diced chicken or sausage patties, stirring to coat. Add curry powder and sea salt and sauté until browned (patties) or cooked (chicken is no longer pink). Combine with veggie curry mixture and stir to coat thoroughly with sauce, or serve in a separate dish so curry remains vegan.

GRAND FIXINGS

Apple and/or pear, chopped (sprinkled with lemon juice to keep from browning)
Red or green grapes, halved
Pomegranate seeds
Bananas, sliced (cut last and kept covered until serving)
Oranges, mandarins, or clementines, sectioned
Caramelized onions
Toasted coconut, shredded (unsweetened)
Dry roasted pistachios
Toasted almonds, sliced
Roasted cashews or peanuts
Yellow raisins or dried cranberries
Dried California apricots
Fresh cilantro, chopped
Scallions, chopped
Fresh basil, chiffonaded

There are many other options besides the ones I've listed here. Use your imagination! Serve curry over a bed of rice, with grand fixings arrayed on the table for everyone to build their own perfect plates.

POTATO LATKES AND FRESH APPLESAUCE

Latkes are potato pancakes, made of shredded potatoes mixed with egg and fried in oil. *Latke* is a Yiddish word derived from the East Slavic word *oladka*, meaning, simply, "small pancake." The Jewish people have been making latkes on Chanukah for hundreds of years. The holiday of Chanukah celebrates the success of the Maccabean revolt, when Jewish freedom fighters reclaimed the Temple from the invading Syrian Greeks. The story goes that after finding the Temple destroyed, the Maccabees wished to reconsecrate it by lighting the ritual menorah. They searched the rubble and could only find one small jug of oil—enough to light the lamp for one night. Somehow, the oil lasted for eight days, and this is the miracle of Chanukah. We cook foods in oil to honor this miracle and to celebrate our perseverance in the face of adversity.

Making latkes on Chanukah is a ritual I have undertaken every year since my kids were very small, although it involved a lot of peeling, grating, crying, and sweating at the stove. And latkes wouldn't be complete without fresh applesauce, right? So, more peeling, coring, and slicing. Still, it was all worth it for the festive feeling that overtook us when we smelled those latkes sizzling. Happily, my relationship with latkes and applesauce was revolutionized in the early 2000s by two pieces of kitchen equipment: I got my first stand mixer with attachments, and suddenly I could coarsely grate a dozen potatoes and four onions in a cool twenty minutes—enough time for someone else to peel, core, and slice a dozen apples. Then that job got easier, too, when I stumbled across an old-fashioned contraption that could peel, core, and slice apples in one shot. As far as I know, it has no technical name beyond "apple peeler-corer-slicer," but this little beauty can be suctioned right onto the counter, allowing for all sorts of fun with apples (see also Tarte aux Pommes—and Serena's perfect illustration below). By now, I've got latkes down to a science, leaving me with time to enjoy our family celebration.

APPLESAUCE

Start the applesauce first so it can cook while you are making latkes. Applesauce is really easy to make—it's only the prep that takes a bit of time. Once in the pot, with just an occasional stir, the apples will very happily turn themselves into sauce.

10 large or 15 med. cooking apples (like Fuji or Braeburn)
1 - 2 Tbsp. raw sugar (or less, if apples are very sweet)
1 tsp. cinnamon
¼ c. water

Peel, core, and slice apples, placing them in a soup pot as you go. Add sugar, cinnamon, and water. Stir once or twice to combine. Turn stove to medium-high, watching that apples don't scorch, and listening for sound of simmering (the water bubbling, the apples letting off steam). Turn heat to medium low so they continue to simmer, checking occasionally. As they cook, they will shrink drastically. Set a timer for every 20 minutes or so, to stir (this helps apples to break down) and to check that nothing is sticking or burning.

Continue cooking for about an hour until apples have completely deconstructed. If desired, mash with a potato masher to eliminate remaining chunks. When it looks like applesauce, it's done. Keep warm.

LATKES

10 large or 15 medium Yukon Gold potatoes
4 large onions
8 eggs, beaten
1 Tbsp. sea salt, or more to taste
Freshly ground black pepper
2 c. vegetable or canola oil for frying, as needed
Sour cream for serving

Using a stand mixer or food processor with a coarse grating attachment, coarsely grate potatoes and onions. (A box grater will do in a pinch—just move slowly so you don't end up grating your knuckles!) Pile batches of grated vegetables in a large colander set into a larger bowl, so they can let their water. Sprinkle each batch with a pinch of salt as you go, to help with the water-letting and flavor the mixture. Press down

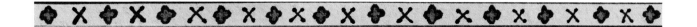

on grated mixture occasionally; you will be amazed at how much liquid comes out. After all potatoes and onions have drained for at least 15 minutes, transfer to a bowl (discard liquid). Add eggs, remainder of salt, and black pepper, mixing thoroughly. (Liquid will continue to accumulate, but you will squeeze as you go.)

You will need an apron, one or two skillets, cookie sheets, paper towels, foil, and plenty of patience. If you are serving the latkes right after you make them, preheat oven to 200 degrees to keep warm as you cook. Cover cookie sheets with foil. Lay out paper towels on a nearby clean work surface to blot latkes as they cook. Set potato mixture next to stove alongside another, smaller empty bowl.

Heat a large skillet or two on medium-high, and pour in enough oil to completely cover the bottom of each skillet. Allow oil to heat briefly. Drop in a bit of latke batter. When it sizzles, you're ready to go.

Take small handfuls of batter, pressing them flat between your hands over smaller bowl to catch liquid. Latkes should be palm-sized and thin. Carefully slide them into skillet without letting your fingers touch oil. If you don't know how to do this without burning yourself, use a spatula! You will get the hang of it.

The first batch of latkes might be light in color and slow to cook, but once the skillet reaches its working temperature, it will be easy to burn them, so keep heat as low as you can without losing the high sizzle. When edges of latkes have crisped and undersides are golden brown, flip with a spatula, watching out for splatters. When they are golden and crispy on both sides, turn down heat and remove carefully but swiftly. Place latkes in a single layer on paper towels, turn over, then transfer to foil-lined cookie sheet. Place in preheated oven. When layer is full, cover with more foil before continuing to stack, to prevent sogginess.

Before starting each batch of latkes, be sure to add more oil to cover bottom of skillet and turn the heat back up a bit so the oil can get hot. This will ensure latkes that are crispy, not greasy.

Repeat steps until all batter is gone. This will take a while even with two pans. Keep adding latkes to oven, so you can serve a platter of them instead of just six at a time that vanish before the next ones are done.

If saving them for another day, top last layer of cookie sheets with more foil and place in freezer. To reheat latkes, preheat oven to 400 degrees, remove pan from freezer, remove top foil, and place sheets directly in oven for 10 to 15 minutes, until latkes are crisp and hot. For crispiest result, separate individual foil layers.

Serve latkes with warm applesauce and cool sour cream. *Makes about 6 to 8 generous servings.*

COOKING TIPS TO LIVE BY

FRESH HERBS AND SPICES

There is a significant difference between fresh herbs and dried ones. While it's true that dried basil, cilantro, parsley, and so on, are less expensive and easier to keep around than their fresh equivalents, the brightness of flavor from fresh herbs is unmatched, and can really be a game-changer in some dishes. If it's within your reach, I urge you to use fresh herbs whenever the recipe calls for them. If you have to substitute, note that the rule of thumb is to use 1 tsp. dried herbs for every Tbsp. of fresh the recipe calls for. Likewise, dried herbs and spices often sit in our spice racks for months or even years, until their essential flavors are only a shadow of what they once were. If a spice features large in a recipe you're planning to cook, take a moment before you shop to assess how long it's been on your shelf, and consider getting a fresh jar—or even better, refill your jar at a bulk store. Your taste buds will thank you.

SIDE DISHES

FAMOUS SQUASH PIE

Perhaps more than any other, this butternut squash pie became the Shabbat dish in our house that everyone asked for and loved. This so-called pie is actually my take on kugel: a savory/sweet casserole that is deeply entrenched in the canon of Eastern European Jewish cooking. The word *kugel* is German for "sphere" or "ball," and the dish—which originated many hundreds of years ago in southern Germany—was so named because a round clay pot or *kugeltopf* was used to keep it moist in the oven. Western Europeans often refer to such a dish as a *schalet*, but *kugel* is what stuck in Eastern Europe. When waves of Jewish immigrants came from there to the New World, they brought the name—and the dish—with them.

This recipe makes two crusts and two squash pies, because one is never enough. A premade pie crust is a shortcut I often use when I am pressed for time; this was especially so with squash pies when the kids were growing up and these pies were perpetually in high demand. But I've added Jeremy's simple pie crust recipe below; of course it always tastes better from scratch! Either way, the crust is a supporting actor in this production, and the fragrant squash filling is the star. The salt is critical here for balancing the pie's sweetness and boosting the mild flavor of the squash, which is lovely on its own but somewhat lacking in dynamism. This squash pie is not quite sweet enough for dessert, but almost! It is a perfect snack, a pretty darn good breakfast, and a delightful accompaniment to veggies, beef, chicken, fish, and…life.

SIMPLE PIE CRUSTS
2 c. unbleached all-purpose flour*
½ tsp. salt
8 Tbsp. cold butter (or margarine)
6 Tbsp. cold water

*For a more nutritious crust, substitute up to two-thirds whole wheat flour; add up to 1 Tbsp. extra water.

Set aside two 9-inch pie pans. In a bowl, combine flour and salt. Cut butter into chunks and add, working with your hands to thoroughly integrate mixture so it looks like damp dirt. Gradually mix in cold water just until dough holds together but is not sticky. Form dough into two balls; place one on a floured surface and use a rolling pin (or wine bottle) to roll it out into a circle just larger than your pie pan. Gently lift circle and lay it over the pan, pressing down so crust settles on bottom. Crimp dough around top of pan and trim excess with a knife. Set aside. Repeat with second ball of dough in second pan. Set aside and make filling.

BUTTERNUT SQUASH FILLING

1 large, fresh butternut squash, or 36 oz. frozen
¼ c. melted butter (or margarine)
¼ c. honey
¼ c. brown sugar, packed
¼ c. water
1 c. unbleached all-purpose flour
4 eggs
1 tsp. salt
Cinnamon for topping

Preheat oven to 350 degrees. If using fresh squash, the easiest way to begin is to steam it whole. Pierce shell with a knife several times and microwave for 8 to 10 minutes, until soft enough to easily pierce with a fork. Remove carefully and allow to cool for several minutes before cutting open with a sharp knife, keeping face away from steam. Allow to cool again until it is safe to handle. Discard seeds, then scoop out orange flesh with a large spoon, placing it in a pot over low heat as you work. Mash squash until smooth.

Another good shortcut—if you want fresh squash but don't want to wrestle with a whole one—is to buy pre-cubed butternut, usually in 20-oz. packages (buy 2). Place in a large pot, cover with water, bring to a boil, reduce heat and cook for a half hour until completely soft. Drain and mash smooth. If using frozen squash, mashed or cubed, heat in a large pot on medium until soft and warmed through.

Stir butter or margarine into mashed hot squash. Whisk in remaining ingredients except cinnamon. Do not leave out the salt! Continue whisking until mixture is smooth and free of lumps. A good potato masher works well, as does an immersion blender. When mixture is smooth and uniformly blended, divide evenly among pie shells. Sprinkle with cinnamon and create a swirl with a butter knife, taking care not to pierce crust.

Bake pies in center of oven for 1 hour. Filling might rise above the crust and separate a bit at the end of baking, but it will settle back down as it cools. Allow at least 15 minutes for pie to cool before serving. If reheating, store in fridge, remove an hour before serving, and warm at low heat (200 degrees), uncovered, so crust does not get soggy. Recipe can easily be doubled for a large gathering. Freezes beautifully, wrapped in foil. *Makes 2 pies; 12 to 16 servings.*

WHOLE-BERRY CRANBERRY SAUCE

Cranberries are indigenous to the bogs and swamps of northeastern North America, and were used by Native American people as a food and a clothing dye for centuries before the colonizers got hold of it. Since sugar didn't arrive in the New World until the late seventeenth century, the first cranberry sauces were likely savory and very tart, but still thickened, since it is the pectin released during cooking that creates their jellied consistency. With the advent of sugar, cranberry sauce came to taste much like the recipe below. The sweeter, more processed canned cranberry sauce was popularized in the 1940s, when widespread industrial canning made out-of-season foods accessible during a time of scarcity. But unlike other canned goods that became pantry staples, jellied cranberry sauce is popular only at Thanksgiving.

The irony of juxtaposing the Native American origin story of cranberry sauce with a mention of the holiday that made it famous is not lost on me. This holiday begs reexamining, as do many of this country's national traditions—a conviction I have repeated with each of my Thanksgiving recipes. It is crucial for us to continue investigating how to make space for these traditions in a more honest and equitable future.

I am notorious for messing up homemade cranberry sauce. It's not exactly complicated—the recipe has three ingredients. And yet, I've been known to throw out two batches in a single go! The problem is that I'm sometimes an impatient cook, and the cranberries must have time enough to release their pectin so they can properly thicken when they cool. Still, I never give up. The homemade stuff is truly glorious, with its ruby-red hue and its intense tart-sweetness; it's a perfect accompaniment to many savory dishes.

1 c. raw or turbinado sugar
1 c. filtered water
2 c. fresh cranberries, rinsed and drained

Bring water and sugar to boil in a saucepan, stirring until sugar is integrated. Drop cranberries into sugar water and bring back to boil, staying by the stove so the mixture does not bubble over. Once boiling, lower to a gentle bubble and cook for 20 minutes, stirring occasionally, until sauce is ruby-red. Pour into a glass bowl and cover, allowing to cool *completely* at room temperature. When totally cooled and already thickening, refrigerate, covered, until one hour before serving. Once it is chilled, it should barely move when you tip the dish. Bring back to room temperature to serve. If doubling recipe, use two separate saucepans. *Makes about 6 to 8 servings.*

CHALLAH STUFFING

The practice of stuffing foods with other foods is so ancient that historians have been unable to trace its origins. The first recorded stuffing recipes date back to a cookbook from the Roman Empire—and even then, there were numerous variations. Over the centuries, a vast range of animals, fruits, and vegetables have been stuffed with an even vaster range of other foods, from wild rice to shellfish to small game birds. Stuffing has historically had many names, too, including "forcemeat," "dressing," and my favorite, "farce."

In our house, stuffing has always meant challah and tarragon. I think the addition of tarragon makes this dish stand out: it is an intense herb with a slightly licorice flavor, so if you've never used it before, be gentle. Homemade challah is unnecessary for this recipe (the stuffing's extensive cooking process would likely obscure your efforts), but try to get an eggy, sweeter loaf, like a brioche. Since I don't make this stuffing inside poultry, it can be made vegetarian by using vegetable stock and olive oil in place of poultry stock or schmaltz. But don't stint on the fat, whatever you choose. Without that, the dish will dry out.

½ c. combo olive oil, schmaltz,* and margarine
2 large or 3 medium sweet onions, diced
1 bunch celery, chopped, with leaves
1 bunch fresh tarragon, chopped, or 1 Tbsp. dried
2 tsp. salt or more to taste
Freshly ground black pepper to taste
3 or 4 c. turkey, chicken, and/or vegetable stock
1 whole challah (not raisin), cut into large cubes

*For easy instructions for rendering schmaltz, see Kasha Varnishkes on page 115.

Preheat oven to 375 degrees. Preheat your largest pot and add 2 Tbsp. fat of your choice. Sauté diced onions until soft and beginning to caramelize, about 15 minutes. Add chopped celery and leaves, chopped tarragon, salt, pepper and 2 more Tbsp. fat, cooking until celery begins to soften. Add enough stock to cover mixture and simmer until very soft and sweet, about 30 to 45 minutes. Turn heat off. Add cubed challah to pot and stir well until bread is entirely coated with broth. Challah should be wet, so add more stock if needed, but not so much that the bread disintegrates. Adjust salt and pepper levels to taste. Spread in large baking pan and dot with remaining fat. Bake for about 30 to 40 minutes until top is golden and crisp. Add a ladle or two of stock or gravy just before serving, or if reheating. *Makes about 10 to 12 servings.*

DUCHESS POTATOES

This is a favorite recipe of Jesse's from his culinary training in Denver, Colorado, where he has been living for several years. These days, we don't get to cook together very much, but when we do, I always end up marveling at whatever he pulls out of his hat. A couple of years ago, I asked him to make a side dish to go with some trout I was pan-frying. He made Duchess Potatoes, which I had never had before. I loved them, which made Jesse happy—and I think he was even happier that he had shown me something new.

Duchess potatoes are a French reinterpretation of mashed potatoes; called *pommes de terre duchesse* in French and *Herzoginkartoffeln* in German, they are spectacular in any language. The familiar mashed potatoes are whipped with egg, Parmesan, and butter, then piped into little potato clouds that turn golden and crisp in the oven. They are a bit fussy to make, but the results speak for themselves: these potatoes are not only elegant (they look a bit like meringues), but they manage to be both light and rich at the same time.

2 lbs. Yukon Gold or Russet potatoes, peeled, cut in half
4 egg yolks
3 oz. (3 Tbsp.) unsalted butter, softened
1 oz. (5 Tbsp.) Parmesan cheese, finely grated
Salt and ground white pepper to taste
1 oz. melted butter for brushing

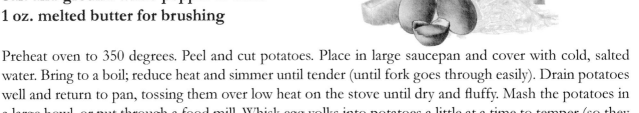

Preheat oven to 350 degrees. Peel and cut potatoes. Place in large saucepan and cover with cold, salted water. Bring to a boil; reduce heat and simmer until tender (until fork goes through easily). Drain potatoes well and return to pan, tossing them over low heat on the stove until dry and fluffy. Mash the potatoes in a large bowl, or put through a food mill. Whisk egg yolks into potatoes a little at a time to temper (so they don't scramble), then add the softened butter, Parmesan, salt, and white pepper, whisking until smooth.

Using a pastry bag with a star tip—or in a pinch, a freezer bag with the end snipped off—pipe 3-inch flowers (or clouds) of the potato mixture onto a parchment-lined sheet pan. Place piped potatoes in oven. After 10 minutes, remove and brush each one with melted butter using a pastry brush. Finish baking until the potatoes are golden brown and heated throughout, about another 5 minutes. If they don't brown, switch oven to broil and move pan to top rack for 1 to 3 minutes, watching so they don't burn. Serve immediately. Fabulous with Swiss-Style Lake Trout or Apricot Chutney-Glazed Salmon. *Makes 12 pieces.*

MIXED ROASTED POTATO WEDGES

This is one of those dishes that can shape-shift easily to suit your needs. The basis of this recipe is a mixture of Yukon Gold and sweet potatoes, roasted in wedges at high heat, with olive oil, dried rosemary, salt, and pepper. Essentially, they are oven fries with the skins on.

It is not necessary to mix them, though: the instructions are the same with only sweet potatoes, or with only yellow potatoes. When I'm using only sweet potatoes, I have been known to sprinkle some cinnamon on. With just yellow potatoes, I add garlic powder and/or smoked paprika. Sometimes I add large chunks of onion to the picture, and let them caramelize. Fresh black pepper finishes the dish no matter what. It's easy, versatile, and pairs with everything—even breakfast.

2 lb. Yukon Gold potatoes
2 lb. sweet potatoes
3 Tbsp. extra virgin olive oil
Fresh or dried rosemary to taste
1 tsp. sea salt, or more to taste
Freshly ground black pepper

Preheat oven to 450 degrees. Wash potatoes and cut into thick wedges by slicing in half the short way, then cutting each half, lengthwise, into three pieces. Place wedges in a big bowl and toss with olive oil, rosemary, salt, and pepper until well coated. Don't stint on the oil or the potatoes will dry out instead of crisping.

Liberally oil two cookie sheets or extra-large baking pans. Spread potatoes on them in a single layer. Put pans side by side on the middle rack of the preheated oven—or if you don't have space for two, place on two racks and switch positions halfway through roasting. Roast for 20 minutes. Remove from oven and use a spatula to turn the wedges so the down sides are now facing up. Return to the oven for another 20 minutes, then test with a fork to be sure they are done, continuing to roast until they are crisp on the outside and soft on the inside. Sweet potatoes will darken more quickly than golds, so watch out for them.

Remove from oven, sprinkle again with salt and pepper, and serve. Pairs beautifully with Apricot Chutney-Glazed Salmon, Shabbat Roast Chicken with Thyme Onion Jam, or Drunken Roast Beef with Herb and Olive Oil Rub. *Makes about 6 to 10 servings.*

CURRIED FRUITED RICE

This recipe is a mash-up of flavors I love: the mild curries of Switzerland (see Vegetable Curry with Grand Fixings for more about this) and the abundant orchard apples and ciders of New England, with a base of aromatic basmati rice. This long-grain rice hails from the Himalayas, but I first found it at an international market in Atlanta. Basmati is sometimes called "popcorn rice" for the distinct aroma and flavor it releases when cooked. Like wine, this aroma varies from year to year depending on soil, weather, and other factors, and—also like wine—the aged varieties of basmati are prized for their depth and complexity.

This dish is terrific when warm, but just as good served cold as a sort of rice salad. In our house it is usually a side, but it could easily be a vegetarian entrée, especially with the addition of protein in the form of chickpeas, lentils, or nuts—almonds, shredded coconut, cashews, or pistachios would go especially well.

4 c. cooked basmati rice
2 Tbsp. extra virgin olive oil
2 Vidalia or other sweet onions, diced
2 apples, peeled, cored, and diced
1 Anjou pear, peeled, cored, and diced
½ c. yellow raisins
1 c. apple cider (or natural apple juice)
1 c. chicken or vegetable broth
1 tsp. sea salt, more as needed
1 Tbsp. mild curry powder
2 Tbsp. honey, more as needed

Cook 2 cups rice in 4 cups water per package directions. Set aside. Preheat large skillet and add oil, letting it liquefy. Add onions and lower to medium, sautéing until soft and golden, 15 to 20 minutes. Add remaining ingredients (except rice). Sauté until fruit is soft, 12 to 15 minutes more. It should be liquidy—if it's not, add more cider and seasoning. Taste, adjusting honey and salt to balance savory, salty, and sweet.

Place cooked rice in large serving dish and pour on contents of skillet, scraping out the bits with a rubber spatula. Stir well to combine, adjusting seasonings for a golden dish bursting with flavor. *Serves 8 to 10.*

CREAMED CAULIFLOWER

The word "cauliflower" comes from the Italian *cavolfiore*, meaning "cabbage flower." It was so named because both cabbage and cauliflower—and several of their cousins like kale, broccoli, Brussels sprouts, and collard greens—come from a single plant species. *Brassica oleracea* first grew in the Mediterranean region as wild mustard; it was cultivated in the gardens of Ancient Greece and Rome, then later in India; centuries of different gardening and farming practices have given rise to its many variations.

When you steam the humble cauliflower until very soft and then cream it in a food processor, it becomes a different thing altogether: smooth and almost starchy, a perfect substitute for the heavier mashed potatoes it comes to resemble. I find—especially when it's warm out—that I prefer this lighter side dish. I love it best as an accompaniment to rainbow trout, barramundi, branzino, and other delicate white fish that I pan sauté with butter and lemon (see Swiss-Style Lake Trout).

1 lg. head cauliflower, cut into big chunks
2 Tbsp. butter or extra virgin olive oil
2 - 4 Tbsp. cream (or nondairy substitute)
¼ to ½ tsp. sea salt, according to taste
Freshly ground black or white pepper to taste

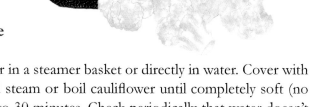

Set a pot of water to boil. Place chunks of cauliflower in a steamer basket or directly in water. Cover with a lid. When water boils, turn down to a simmer, and steam or boil cauliflower until completely soft (no resistance when you pierce it with a fork), about 25 to 30 minutes. Check periodically that water doesn't boil out; scorching will affect the dish's flavor. Use a slotted spoon to remove soft cauliflower from pot.

Transfer cauliflower into a food processor in two batches. (Mashing by hand will not achieve the same silky texture as a food processor, though a blender will do.) Add 1 Tbsp. of the butter and a good pinch salt with each batch. With motor on, pour 1 Tbsp. cream or unsweetened milk substitute through spout, adding more as needed, depending on how thick you want it to be. I like it quite thick. When it looks smooth, turn off food processor and use rubber spatula (not your hand!) to be sure there are no lumps.

Transfer to a covered casserole dish and repeat with second batch. Add ground black or white pepper and more salt to taste. Cover until ready to serve. Keeps in fridge for several days. *Serves 4 to 6.*

KASHA VARNISHKES

When I was growing up, my parents spoke rapturously about kasha varnishkes, an iconic Ashkenazi Jewish dish that hails from Eastern Europe, where almost all of our ancestors came from. Kasha (also known as buckwheat groats—which, incidentally, contain no wheat) is extremely nutritious and packs about 13 grams of protein into every hundred grams of grain. So it can easily be a vegetarian main dish. And what are *varnishkes*, you might be wondering? Derived from the Ukrainian word *vareniki*, they are simply rectangular noodles or "dumplings" mixed with the kasha. Older iterations of this dish included dumplings stuffed with kasha, but in recent decades, it has become commonplace to mix the kasha with bow tie noodles. Kasha by itself is pretty bland, but here it is elevated by the addition of caramelized onions and noodles, not to mention plenty of salt and fat.

The liberal use of fat—originally schmaltz or rendered chicken fat—is a key to this dish, as it helps flavor and caramelize the onions and ensures that the kasha and bow ties do not dry out. If you want to use schmaltz, I recommend you do so for half the fat in this recipe (2 - 3 Tbsp.), and make up the rest with some extra virgin olive oil. If you want to keep the dish vegetarian or vegan, olive oil or butter will do nicely. The other key is the treatment of the kasha: before being cooked in water, it is toasted in a dry pan, sealing the groats and releasing their nutty aroma; then, after cooking, it is re-toasted in the skillet with the onions and fat, making the kasha crunchy and turning it a deep, golden brown.

Follow all of the steps below to achieve the full effect of this dish.

4 - 6 Tbsp. schmaltz and/or olive oil
2 large, sweet onions, chopped
At least 1 tsp. salt, or more to taste
1½ c. boiling water
¾ c. kasha (buckwheat groats)
1 egg, beaten
Freshly ground black pepper to taste
½ pound bow ties or egg noodles, al dente

RENDERING SCHMALTZ (THE EASY WAY)

Roast a cut-up kosher chicken (skin on), covered with foil, in a 450-degree oven until juices run clear, about an hour. When cool enough to handle, shred chicken to use elsewhere (try the Creamy Curried Chicken Salad!) and pour drippings into a heatproof jar or cup. Place in fridge until cold and separated. The hardened top layer of white fat is the schmaltz. Save the liquid layer for soup stock, storing in fridge.

CARAMELIZING ONIONS

Put 2 Tbsp. schmaltz and/or oil in skillet and heat on medium-high. Add chopped onions and a pinch of salt, cooking until onions become translucent. Turn heat to medium low and continue cooking, stirring occasionally, until onions are very soft, golden brown, and greatly reduced in volume, adding 1 Tbsp. additional fat if needed. Be patient; this takes about 30 minutes. Turn off heat, leaving onions in skillet.

PREPARING PASTA

While onions are cooking, bring a large pot of liberally salted water to boil for bow tie pasta. Cook noodles until just al dente (tender but firm). Drain pasta and place in a serving bowl, topping immediately with 1 Tbsp. oil or schmaltz. Add salt and black pepper to taste. Stir until pasta is well coated. Set aside.

COOKING KASHA

Bring 1½ c. water to a boil. Mix **dry** kasha in a small bowl with the beaten egg. Preheat an empty saucepan to medium-high and stir in the kasha-egg mixture. Toast until kasha is golden and dry, about 5 minutes. Wearing a long oven mitt and keeping your face well away, add the 1½ c. boiling water to saucepan (it will bubble up angrily for a moment and then settle down). Stir in ½ tsp. salt. Cover tightly and simmer until kasha is soft and fluffy, about 10 minutes.

Combine kasha with caramelized onions in skillet, adding another 1 to 2 Tbsp. oil if there isn't much visible fat remaining in pan. Turn heat to medium-high and stir until all is blended and kasha browns and crisps in the oil. Don't remove from heat until some bits of kasha have turned dark and the whole thing is just shy of burning—you will know it's done from the toasty aroma. The whole house will! Stir in the bow ties, giving it all a good mix so the pasta is coated with bits of caramelized onions, fat, and kasha.

Return mixture to serving bowl, adding more salt and pepper to taste—this dish is best with lots of both—and serve immediately. Marvelous with Shabbat Roast Chicken with Thyme Onion Jam and some lightly sautéed green cabbage (see Inside-Out Stuffed Cabbage). Worthy of a *shtetl* wedding. *Serves 6 to 10.*

CREMINI MUSHROOMS IN BUTTER WITH RED WINE, THYME, AND GARLIC

This recipe blends several culinary loves of mine into one simple but spectacular dish. Sautéing mushrooms in butter and wine feels decadent: one bite with my eyes closed and I am transported to the French Riviera, where I spent some time as a teen. The French are quite talented at working alcohol into all sorts of dishes, from Boeuf Bourguignon to Crepes Suzette, and I love them all. But this one wins for ease of preparation.

I like to use Baby Bellas, also known as cremini mushrooms, for this recipe: they are young portabella mushrooms, a variety native to Italy that has been growing there for centuries. Portabellas become quite large in adulthood, and so they are wonderful for grilling; they can be treated almost like steaks, and their meaty flavor often serves as a stand-in for beef among vegetarians. Even the younger Baby Bellas have a more robust flavor than white mushrooms and stand up very nicely to the aggressiveness of the red wine.

This simple but elegant preparation has a special place in my heart because the combination of flavors is so rich and complex, but also because it reminds me of my father: he loved very few vegetables, but he had a passion for mushrooms—and taught me almost everything I know about wine. Here's to you, Poppi.

2 lbs. cremini (Baby Bella) mushrooms, quartered
2 Tbsp. butter (or olive oil if non-dairy)
1 Tbsp. extra virgin olive oil
3 cloves garlic, minced
6 sprigs fresh thyme (or 1 tsp. dried)
1 c. dry red wine, or more to taste
¼ tsp. sea salt, or more to taste
Freshly ground black pepper to taste

Wipe mushrooms gently with a damp cloth to remove lingering dirt. Trim rough stems so they are even, and quarter mushrooms: turn them on their backs, slicing in half right through the stems, then adjust their position to repeat in the other direction. This shape makes a more substantial variation from flat slices.

Preheat a heavy-bottom skillet to medium-high. Melt 1 Tbsp. butter and the olive oil, allowing them to run together. Add minced garlic, browning just until fragrant (be careful not to burn) before adding mushrooms. Turn heat down to medium, sautéing until mushrooms begin to soften and let some of their liquid, about 5 to 7 minutes.

Strip thyme sprigs from their stems, chop fine, and add to pan. (Discard stems.) Pour in red wine and stir to coat mushrooms with the herbs and liquid, cooking at a high enough temperature that wine begins to reduce. Continue until wine is reduced by half, probably 2 to 4 minutes or so. Turn heat off, add last Tbsp. butter along with salt and pepper. Taste and adjust seasonings to your liking.

These little beauties can be paired with so many things: Pasta Puttanesca and Sesame Crusted Tuna Steak come to mind; but they complement beef especially well, and with Drunken Roast Beef and Duchess Potatoes they could very possibly bring you to tears. *Serves 6 to 8*.

HARICOTS VERTS WITH TOASTED ONIONS

I love haricots verts (pronounced "AH-ree-koh VARE," also called French green beans) because they are thinner, more intensely flavored, and sweeter than conventional green beans. All green beans are simply the immature fruit of the common bean, picked before their protective husks become tough—and haricots verts are harvested even earlier in the growing season, when they are still tender and light green. The dried minced onions (found in most every grocer's spice section), if toasted but not burned, create the perfect savory accompaniment to the flavorful beans.

1 Tbsp. extra virgin olive oil
1 Tbsp. butter (or olive oil if non-dairy)
1½ lbs. haricots verts (or green beans, if not available)
Sea salt and black pepper to taste
2 Tbsp. dried minced onions

Heat the olive oil and butter in a heavy-bottom skillet on high. Wash and trim the beans so no hard stems remain. Add to the oil and turn down to medium-high. As the beans turn bright green, add salt and pepper.

When beans begin browning a bit on the edges, add the dried onions, stirring and tossing frequently. The onions will brown quickly, and you want to toast them without burning them or they will become bitter. When they are golden brown and fragrant, and the beans are still bright green and have just begun to soften, remove skillet from heat and transfer immediately to a serving dish. Serve hot.

Delicious as an accompaniment to any number of dishes. Two of my favorites are Apricot-Chutney Glazed Salmon and Chicken with Roasted Garlic, Potatoes, Lemon, and Tomatoes. *Serves 4 to 6.*

PAN-ROASTED ASPARAGUS WITH GARLIC AND SEA SALT

Springtime means asparagus, the simplest and most elegant of green vegetables. When they are fresh and in season, they are unbeatable, with their delicate flavor and tender floral tips. I like asparagus best when they are cooked fast, in a hot pan, with just a bit of olive oil and butter. Somehow this preparation brings out their natural sweetness, and renders this dish one of the quickest and easiest sides you can make.

1½ lbs. fresh, thick asparagus
1 Tbsp. extra virgin olive oil
2 cloves garlic, minced
1 Tbsp. butter (or extra Tbsp. oil)
½ tsp. sea salt, or more to taste
Freshly ground black pepper to taste

Rinse and pat asparagus dry. Bend each stalk from the thick end until it snaps, discarding the broken end, even if it is a third of the stalk. Just think of that part as inedible, like the husk of a corn cob or a fruit pit. This is a good way to ensure that the asparagus will be tender instead of stringy and tough.

Preheat large, heavy-bottom skillet on high, then add oil and allow a minute for it to liquefy. Carefully place asparagus spears in pan, all facing the same direction if possible, and turn heat to medium-high. Allow spears to brown on one side, 2 to 3 minutes, then give the pan a good shake or use tongs to roll them over a bit so they brown on their undersides.

When spears have turned from dull to bright green, add the garlic, tossing frequently with asparagus so it doesn't burn. Pan roasting should take a total of 5 to 7 minutes, until the spears can be pierced with a fork at the thicker end but still offer some resistance. In the last two minutes, add butter or extra oil and shake pan once mores so it gets to the undersides of the asparagus. Sprinkle liberally with sea salt and grind some black pepper over the top. Asparagus should still be bright green, with some brown pan marks showing. Adjust seasonings as needed. Lovely as an accompaniment to chicken, fish, or pasta (see especially Green Goddess Pasta). Also perfect for breakfast alongside Four-Minute Eggs. *Serves 4 to 6.*

COOKING TIPS TO LIVE BY

"TO TASTE"

In this cookbook, you will find that I often list seasonings and other ingredients "to taste," which rightly implies that you should be tasting your food as it cooks. This is imperative for your success as a home cook. There is no other way to know whether you like the way the dish tastes before you serve it—or whether it needs some course correction. Even with baking, I recommend tasting your batter or filling once or twice—and if your kids are in the kitchen with you, I'm sure they'll be glad to help. I can't tell you how often this has saved me from accidentally omitting a crucial ingredient—like salt—or given me that extra chance to tweak a recipe. But don't take my word for it. Experiment! I will always let you know when an element in a recipe is indispensable or shouldn't be substituted. For everything else, it will not take you long to figure out what works and what doesn't. Trust your taste buds, familiarize yourself with a range of flavors, and you will find that these dishes soon become your own.

KIDS' FAVORITES

MIMI'S FARM EGGS

Dairy in Switzerland is always deliciously fresh and reasonably priced, because—even in the cities—the nearest farm is only a short drive away. My mother's Farm Eggs, a dish my siblings and I loved as children and that I have carried with me through all the years since, was a culinary invention born out of those simple pleasures, with her own little American twist: eggs poached in butter and milk with crushed corn flakes on top. This quartet might sound odd, but I assure you the sum here is more than the parts. The butter crisps the edges of the eggs, the milk balances their richness, and the corn flakes add a lovely color and texture—some of them stay crunchy, and some soak up the milk and turn into a delicious mess. Start with real butter and use the freshest eggs and milk you can find.

2 Tbsp. butter
4 eggs, pref. free-range
1½ c. milk, pref. whole, more as needed
¼ c. cornflakes, lightly crushed
Salt and pepper to taste

Place butter in a nonstick skillet on medium-high heat, and melt. Break eggs carefully into pan, keeping yolks intact. Cook in the butter for a minute or two, until the whites just begin to turn opaque and the edges begin to crisp.

Pour milk into skillet, adjusting amount so eggs are surrounded with liquid and almost completely covered (but not quite), with the yolks peeking up from the surface. Bring milk to a bubble, then turn to medium low so that milk continues bubbling gently without scorching. Salt and pepper the eggs lightly and allow to cook until the yolk feels warm to the touch of your fingertip or knuckle.

Sprinkle crushed corn flakes on top and continue to cook another 1 to 3 minutes, until eggs are "medium" (yolks are beginning to firm up but are still somewhat runny); add a bit of milk if it has reduced a lot.

Using a rubber spatula, loosen the edges of the milky cornflake mixture and slide the whole ensemble onto a plate. Don't leave the milky stuff behind! *Serves 4 kids or 2 adults.*

FROG IN A HOLE

These little delights came from David, who always loved camping, and hailed Frogs in a Hole as the perfect one-pan breakfast. In case you were wondering, they have nothing whatsoever to do with frogs; they are simply eggs over easy nestled into skillet toast. A Frog in a Hole takes only a few minutes to make and requires very little attention, though it's important to try to keep the yolk from breaking. As you might imagine, I have eaten an impressive number of broken-yoke froggies in my day. The fun of this dish for kids is finding the beautiful sunny eggs, whole and shining, in the midst of their bread nests.

4 slices soft multigrain bread
2 Tbsp. butter
4 eggs, pref. free-range
Salt
Pepper

Use an upside down shot glass to punch a hole out of the middle of each slice of bread, or pinch out a yolk-sized hole with your fingers. Set aside bread rounds to fry up later.

Melt butter in a large nonstick skillet on medium-high until bubbling. Place two slices of bread in skillet and brown slightly for 2 to 3 minutes on bottom. Flip bread over and break an egg carefully over the hole in the middle of each slice, aiming the yolk into the hole. Allow to cook until whites begin to turn opaque, using a spatula to lift the bread once or twice so uncooked whites can reach the heat. This is a good time to pop the bread rounds into the pan with a little extra butter. Using a wide spatula, gingerly flip each slice of bread over, trying not to break the yolk. (Flip the little bread rounds as well.) Sprinkle with salt and fresh black pepper. Once the whites have all turned opaque, remove to a plate and cover loosely with foil while you repeat with the second batch. *Makes 4 servings.* Can be infinitely multiplied.

FOUR-MINUTE EGGS

This dish is not so much about the recipe as it is about the experience of eating a soft-boiled egg in a beautiful ceramic egg cup. When I was a small girl in Switzerland, we always had a collection of these cups, colorfully painted and waiting patiently for breakfast on a shelf in the kitchen. My mother would make us four-minute eggs, and set them in their cups in front of us so we could crack the shells ourselves and spoon out the warm, eggy goodness. These cups were tiny works of art (as you can see in Serena's perfect illustrations below.) Thirty years after I left, when I finally took my kids to see where I had been born, I bought them each an egg cup to take home and started making them four-minute eggs for breakfast, too.

In America, most egg yolks are pale yellow; eggs here are largely produced in industrial chicken coops, where corn is the feed of choice because it's readily available and, therefore, less expensive. Hens in Europe are almost always free-range, so they feed on a natural diet of grasses—which contain beta carotene—making their yolks more orange than yellow. In fact, this vibrant orange color is so prized that European egg farmers often mix marigold leaves, orange peels, carrots, and other natural sources of beta carotene into the hens' feed to produce a more intensely colored yolk.

4 eggs, pref. free-range
Egg cups
Salt to sprinkle

Fill a small saucepan three-fourths full of water and bring to a boil. Using a slotted spoon, carefully place eggs in water so they don't crack. Set a timer for exactly 4 minutes. When time is up, remove eggs immediately with slotted spoon and stand them in egg cups. Crack the sides of the shell with a teaspoon and flip the top off like a lid, creating just enough space to dip the spoon in. Sprinkle with salt and enjoy!
Makes 4 servings.

SERENA'S "NOONIES" (NOODLES WITH BUTTER AND PARMESAN)

Parmigiano Reggiano, which I use in many of my recipes, is rightfully called the King of Cheeses. This granular, intensely-flavored hard cheese originated almost a thousand years ago, with a group of Benedictine and Cistercian monks from Italy's Parma-Reggio region who were determined to develop a cheese with a long natural shelf life. As befits a cheese whose first sale can be traced back to 1200, the name and process of making Parmigiano Reggiano are enshrined in Italian law and throughout the European Union as "protected designations of origin,"; the cheese's full name and even the label "Parmesan" can only be used to refer to the authentically-made product. This law is less strict in the US, but still, only cheese made according to the proper process and aged between 12 and 36 months can be called "Parmesan." With its unique trove of tiny, salty crystals and its undeniable umami flavor, even a small amount of freshly grated Parmigiano Reggiano has the power to transform the simplest dish into something special.

This is, in fact, the simplest of kid-friendly dishes—and one that Serena lived on almost exclusively for months (possibly years) of her young life. But even a dish like this can be an opportunity to introduce young ones to the chewy texture of al dente pasta, the distinctive bite of black pepper, and the sharp, nutty flavor of freshly grated Parmigiano Reggiano.

In Serena's immortal words, "Noonies are good!"

NOONIES
8 oz. short noodles, like penne or bow ties
1 tsp. butter for each serving (1 - 2 Tbsp. total)
Salt and freshly ground black pepper
Freshly grated Parmigiano Reggiano

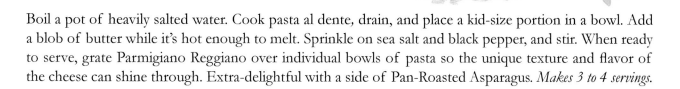

Boil a pot of heavily salted water. Cook pasta al dente, drain, and place a kid-size portion in a bowl. Add a blob of butter while it's hot enough to melt. Sprinkle on sea salt and black pepper, and stir. When ready to serve, grate Parmigiano Reggiano over individual bowls of pasta so the unique texture and flavor of the cheese can shine through. Extra-delightful with a side of Pan-Roasted Asparagus. *Makes 3 to 4 servings.*

GABY SANDWICH (CREAM CHEESE, CINNAMON-SUGAR, AND BANANAS)

This was my oldest daughter Gabriella's earliest culinary invention, one that, in its many variations, became popular with all the kids. The "Gaby Sandwich" was the first of our cookie cutter sandwiches, made with soft bread and assorted fillings, then cut into fun shapes with cookie cutters. This method lends itself to nearly endless variety: the favorites in our house were star sandwiches. It gives me great pleasure to realize that my grandson, Asher, is nearly at the age when he will be able to enjoy his mama's childhood creation.

One more fun fact: did you know that bananas grow in such a way that they can naturally be sectioned into thirds the long way? These sections are called *locules,* and bananas are "trilocular." If you slice off the banana's tip and gently push your thumb into the flat surface, it will split neatly into three down the whole length of the fruit. I am nearly giddy at the prospect of showing this trick to Asher for the first time, just as soon as he is old enough to appreciate how cool it really is.

8 slices soft whole wheat bread
8 oz. cream cheese
2 just-ripe bananas
Cinnamon sugar to taste*

*You can make cinnamon sugar at home with 1 tsp. cinnamon to every ¼ c. raw sugar, and store it in a jar for next time you need it.

Spread cream cheese lightly on one side of all 8 pieces of bread. Slice banana into wheels or divide into sections as above, and arrange in a single layer on top of cream cheese on four of the slices. Sprinkle generously with cinnamon sugar and set other cream-cheesed bread on top.

Push sandwiches together gently so the two halves adhere. Use cookie cutters to cut out as much of each sandwich as possible. Scraps can be artfully sliced into tiny bites so they are not wasted.

Serves about 3 or 4 hungry kids.

Below are other good fillings for the Gaby Sandwich. Don't forget the cookie cutters!

HOPPED-UP PBJ
Peanut butter or almond butter with jam or honey and banana or apple slices

APPLE-AND-CHOCOLATE-A-DAY
Nutella with thin apple slices

CALIFORNIAN
Mashed avocado with cheese and tomatoes

MIDDLE EASTERN
Hummus with cucumbers and/or sweet peppers

EUROPEAN
Boursin (or other soft herb cheese) with salted and peppered tomatoes

SOPHISTICATED
Spreadable goat cheese with lox, slivers of red onion, and cucumbers

REAL MAC 'N' CHEESE

The first macaroni and cheese recipes date back to the late thirteenth century in southern Italy—but you wouldn't be wrong to think of it as an American food, given how ubiquitous it has become since the Kraft company first patented its powdered cheese mix and put it in a box with some elbow macaroni in 1937. It was tasty and cost 19 cents, so during World War II, that box became a staple in American households.

Indeed, my earliest experiences of mac 'n' cheese revolved around those boxes, found at the house of my childhood friend, Laura, whose Italian family had enthusiastically adopted many American conveniences. This is one of my happiest memories of middle school, a time that offers few comforts for most kids: riding to Laura's house on the school bus, our stomachs inevitably grumbling, we'd fling down our backpacks in the hallway, kick off our shoes, and cook up a mess of the fluorescent orange stuff, eating it on the couch in the living room as we wriggled our bare toes in the blue pile carpet. It was the best thing ever.

This homemade mac 'n' cheese bears little resemblance to the boxed version beyond its undisputed role as a comfort food. It's more nutritious but not nearly as quick, since it has a creamy Mornay sauce as its base. This is a classic French sauce, a cheesy bechamel; actually, bechamel's older sibling, invented by Duke Philippe de Mornay in the late sixteenth century. For my recipe, Mornay's traditional Gruyere is replaced with cheddar, mozzarella, and Parmesan for an Italian-American twist—a fitting tribute to my old friend.

Still, the whole process takes less time than you'd think, and the result is something special: the velvety, creamy sauce clings happily to the curved elbows, the cheddar and Parmigiano provide a sharp, nutty contrast, and the delicate, oven-toasted breadcrumbs send the whole thing into the stratosphere.

MAC 'N' CHEESE
1 lb. elbow macaroni
1 recipe Mornay sauce (see below)
8 oz. grated mozzarella, divided
8 oz. grated sharp cheddar, divided
3 oz. grated Parmigiano Reggiano
½ c. panko or Italian breadcrumbs
Salt and black pepper to taste

Set a pot of well-salted water to boil. Grate and divide cheeses for both Mornay sauce and topping. Begin making sauce (below) while waiting for water to boil. Cook pasta until it's on the firm side of al dente (slightly underdone); it will soften further in the oven. Drain, rinse, and place in bowl. Assemble as below.

MORNAY SAUCE
6 c. whole milk
½ tsp. salt
Generous pinch white pepper
8 Tbsp. unsalted butter, plus more for casserole dish
8 Tbsp. unbleached all-purpose flour
4 oz. grated sharp cheddar (from 8 oz. on prev. page)
4 oz. grated mozzarella cheese (from 8 oz. on prev. page)

Combine milk with salt and white pepper in a saucepan. Heat on medium, watching carefully so it does not burn. When milk begins to steam and bubbles form at edges, turn way down and keep warm.

Preheat a skillet to medium. Melt butter, then sprinkle in flour and whisk vigorously until you create a smooth paste called a *roux*. Let the roux bubble for one minute as you continue whisking. Add ½ c. of the seasoned warm milk, a little at a time, whisking constantly to eliminate lumps. It will seize up at first, but don't worry! As you add more and more warm milk and keep whisking it into the roux, it will smooth out into a slurry. When it is smooth and thin enough to pour, add it back to remainder of the warm milk, whisking to combine and stirring as it thickens, 5 to 10 minutes, until it leaves a thick white coat on a wooden spoon. Drop in 4 oz. each of grated cheddar and mozzarella cheeses, stirring until melted and creamy. Keep Mornay sauce on very low heat, stirring regularly until ready to use.

Preheat oven to 350 degrees. Butter a large casserole dish, at least 9 x 13 in. with deep sides. Pour warm Mornay sauce over bowl of macaroni, stirring until it is thoroughly coated. Transfer mixture to casserole dish and spread into an even layer. Sprinkle with 4 oz. each of additional grated mozzarella and cheddar cheeses, then top with grated Parmigiano Reggiano and breadcrumbs. Bake for 30 to 40 minutes, until top is golden and sauce is bubbling around the edges. Allow to cool for at least 10 minutes before serving. *Makes about 6 to 8 servings as a main dish.*

Perfect with an All-Green Salad as a meal, or serve both as accompaniments to Swiss-Style Lake Trout.

PANINI WITH FRESH MOZZARELLA, ARUGULA, AND RASPBERRIES

This is by far the loveliest grilled cheese I have ever seen. The original idea for this recipe came from celebrity chef Giada De Laurentiis, whose concept of mixing raspberry jam with fresh mozzarella and rosemary in a sandwich I fell in love with years ago. Since then I've tweaked a few things here and there, substituting multigrain for white bread and adding fresh raspberries and arugula to the mix for a more textured and nutritious final result, but the original credit is hers. The rosemary intensifies the lovely floral notes of the raspberries, and the brown sugar, added near the end of the cooking process, creates a glorious crust on the outside of the bread as it mixes with the olive oil in the heat. This is one of those sandwiches that works equally well for breakfast, brunch, or lunch—it is a standby when my kids visit.

My friend Jeremy, with whom I've spent many happy hours in the kitchen, taught me that a perfect grilled cheese depends on timing: you want to melt the cheese completely before the bread gets too dark. In order to accomplish this feat, you have to do two things: first, bring the cheese up to room temperature before assembling your sandwiches, and second, turn the sandwiches over several times in the skillet (instead of just once) so that the heat on each surface never gets too high. I find that if I follow his suggestions with any form of grilled cheese, I have a perfectly melted sandwich on evenly-toasted bread every time.

8 oz. fresh mozzarella, room temperature
½ c. seedless red raspberry fruit spread
1 c. fresh raspberries
8 even slices fresh multigrain bread from a large loaf
¼ c. extra virgin olive oil
2 sprigs fresh rosemary, chopped (or 1 tsp. dried)
1. c. fresh arugula
2 Tbsp. brown sugar

Cut mozzarella log into thick slices and bring to room temperature. Warm raspberry fruit spread in microwave for about 30 seconds, then mix gently in a small bowl with fresh raspberries, trying not to bruise them as you stir to coat.

Line up the bread on a clean surface and, using a pastry brush, paint one side of each piece of bread liberally with olive oil. Turn bread over and make sure the pieces line up so that they work together as sandwiches. On four of the slices of bread, place pieces of fresh mozzarella and add a small handful of arugula. On the other four, spread a liberal layer of raspberry mixture and sprinkle rosemary over the top.

Preheat panini pan while you assemble sandwiches. If you don't have a panini maker, use a good nonstick skillet and a heavy lid (or, in a pinch, the bottom of a second skillet). It won't have those fun panini ridges, but it will still taste just as wonderful. Press sandwich halves together with the oily sides out. Place assembled sandwiches on preheated panini pan; they will immediately sizzle if the pan is hot enough. Once you've achieved a good sizzle, turn the heat down to medium.

Remember Jeremy's trick (see previous page): you will want to flip the sandwiches several times to control the temperature of the bread as you melt the cheese. I find that setting a timer and turning the sandwiches every 60 to 90 seconds, for a total of three times on each side, works best. The panini maker or skillet will also continue to accumulate heat, so you will likely have to turn it down to low before you are done.

When cheese is just about all melted and you are on the last flip, sprinkle the brown sugar evenly over the top sides of the sandwiches. Press down the panini lid for a minute or two, being careful not to burn the sugar as it melts and forms a crunchy, sweet layer on the bread. Remove to a plate, cut into halves diagonally, and serve immediately to exclamations of delight. *Makes 8 large sandwich halves.*

MUESLI AND FROGURT

Muesli or Müsli—a word that essentially means mash-up or "little porridge"—hails from my childhood in Zurich, where it was invented around the turn of the twentieth century by a doctor named Maximilian Bircher-Benner. His original recipe—which consisted of oat flakes, raw apples, condensed milk, nuts, and lemon juice—was said to have effected a miraculous cure in many of his patients. Starting in the 1950s, the dry ingredients were packaged and sold to the public as *Birchermuesli*; it was still touted as a health food but the recipe had changed to include dried fruit; the lemon juice had vanished; and the condensed milk was eventually replaced with regular milk or yogurt at home. It was a bit like a glorified granola, except that the oats were always raw, and it was almost always served with grated raw apple. Sometimes the oat mixture was left in yogurt or milk overnight in the fridge so that it turned soft, and then the fresh fruit was added just before serving. That's how I remember it best.

When I was a girl, we used to go for a family treat to Café Select in Zurich, and I always ordered the Müsli there: they served it in a huge parfait glass, with peaches and whipped cream. A far cry from Dr. Bircher-Benner's tonic, but I loved it.

Decades later, "muesli" began to appear in the grocery sections of American supermarkets, but it never tasted the way I remembered, and so I began to make it myself. The recipe below contains a lot of ingredients, but since most of them are dry and non-perishable, the muesli can be mixed in great batches and stored in an airtight container in the pantry.

When all of my kids were little, there were times when even mixing a batch of muesli seemed to be a bridge too far, and so instead I just made "frogurt" (fruit + yogurt) out of dried nuts and fruit mixed with yogurt and grated apple for a quick, filling meal. It's one that Gabriella still counts among her favorites, and that I eat on most days in the summer, too. I have included that simpler variation here as well. Either way, have fun with the possibilities! They are only limited by the season and your imagination.

MUESLI

This recipe makes a big batch; can be halved or quartered as desired. *Makes about 20 to 25 servings.*

6 c. rolled oats (not instant or steel-cut)
½ c. yellow raisins
½ c. dried cranberries (or dried currants)
1 c. dried California apricots, snipped with scissors
1 - 2 c. chopped hazelnuts, walnuts, and/or almonds
½ c. sunflower or pumpkin seeds
2 - 4 Tbsp. brown sugar, to taste
1 tsp. cinnamon

Place all ingredients in a giant bowl, mixing until they are fully integrated. Store in a cannister until ready to use. Keeps for up to 3 months in a dry, cool place.

To serve: For each helping, mix ¼ to ½ c. **muesli** with **1 c. yogurt** of your choice. If too thick, stir in enough **milk** to loosen mixture until desired consistency is reached. **Grate ½ peeled apple** directly into bowl; add **any other fresh fruit** you'd like. Berries and peaches are especially good. Muesli is also tasty as a cold cereal with just milk and fruit, and it can easily be cooked into a hearty oatmeal in colder weather.

FROGURT

2 c. yogurt, any flavor
2 peeled firm apples, grated large
Fresh berries or other fresh fruit, as desired
3 or 4 dried California apricot halves, snipped
¼ c. chopped walnuts, almonds, and/or hazelnuts
¼ c. dried cranberries and/or golden raisins
Fresh fruit and/or berries as desired

Place yogurt in a large bowl. Peel apple and grate into yogurt. Snip dried apricots; chop nuts. Mix both into yogurt along with raisins or craisins and any fresh fruit or berries you want. Serve immediately. Adjust proportions as needed. *Makes about 4 to 6 servings.*

COOKING TIPS TO LIVE BY

AVOID OVERBAKING

I frequently warn against *overbaking* and *overcooking*, because doing so can really undermine your efforts in the kitchen. My approach is not always conventional: for example, unlike many recipes that direct you to remove your baked goods from the oven when a tester or toothpick inserted in the center comes out "clean," I suggest you do so when there are still crumbs clinging to the tester. Of course, you don't want to see a smear of raw batter there, but a bit of clinging crumb is absolutely key to a moist cake. Likewise, a salmon fillet should come out of the oven *before* it turns pale all the way through, as it will continue to cook when it's been removed from the heat. My recipes offer a range of cooking and baking times to account for the fact that every oven and stove works differently, and I encourage you to experiment with yours to find the right balance. But here is a good rule of thumb: if it feels like it's *almost* done, it's done.

CONFECTIONS

VANILLA EGG CUSTARD

The magical vanilla bean is a pod derived from orchids that originated in Central and South America and the Caribbean. The Totonac tribe in the mountains of Mexico were the first to cultivate vanilla pods, but used them for medicinal and religious purposes, believing they were a sacred gift. The word "vanilla," or in Spanish, *vainilla,* is a diminutive of the Spanish word *vaina*, and simply means "little pod."

Custards (puddings made with eggs) feature in a nearly endless variety of dishes: as a medium for savory pies (like Summer Corn Tart), as the basis of a sweet treat (see Chocolate Challah Bread Pudding, Lemon Custard Bars, and Crème Caramel), or as a stand-alone dessert like this one. My mother used to give me vanilla custard whenever I was sick at home, so for me, it will always have magical healing powers.

This lovely custard cooks entirely on the stove and comes together in less than half an hour, smooth and creamy on the tongue, not too rich or too sweet, and infused with the comforting fragrance of vanilla.

3 c. whole milk
Scant ½ c. sugar
½ tsp. salt
1 tsp. quality vanilla extract
3 tbsp. cornstarch
2 Tbsp. butter
4 egg yolks

In a saucepan, whisk together all ingredients except egg yolks, and cook on medium, stirring almost constantly to prevent milk from sticking to pan. Continue until small bubbles form and steam is rising from the surface (not quite boiling) and it is beginning to thicken up. Remove from heat.

In a bowl, beat 4 egg yolks until light and frothy, about 1 minute. (See Sublime Chocolate Mousse for instructions on how to separate eggs.) Whisk in half of hot milk mixture a bit at a time to temper the eggs without scrambling. Pour egg mixture into pan with rest of milk. Keeping flame low, reheat custard, stirring constantly until it coats a rubber spatula thickly, about 3 to 5 minutes. Pour into a dish and place saran wrap directly on surface of custard to prevent a milk-skin from forming. Refrigerate 30 minutes to serve warm; 3 hours to serve chilled. Divine with raspberries and whipped cream. *Makes 6 to 8 servings.*

LEMON CUSTARD BARS

Lemon bars are a particular favorite of my mother's, and I am always happy to make her a batch. There are a thousand-and-one tiny variations of the well-loved lemon bar, a custardy confection with a shortbread base. I must have tried a hundred of them. But the ones we both love most are on the tangy side, with the lemon making itself heard loud and clear rather than being eclipsed by the sugar. The trouble is, if you add too much lemon juice, the custard will not hold its shape. In other words—as with so many rewarding undertakings—a balance must be struck. This recipe reflects years of happy tinkering with that balance.

SHORTBREAD CRUST
1½ c. unbleached all-purpose flour, sifted
½ c. confectioners' sugar, sifted
¾ c. butter (or margarine)
¼ tsp. salt

Preheat oven to 350 degrees; grease a 9-inch square pan. Use hands or a dough hook to work all ingredients together until they form a dough. Press evenly into bottom of pan. Bake for 25 minutes, until golden around the sides. While crust is baking, make lemon custard.

LEMON CUSTARD
3 large eggs, beaten
6 Tbsp. freshly squeezed lemon juice
Scant 1 c. granulated raw sugar
½ tsp. baking powder
¼ tsp. salt
2 Tbsp. flour, sifted (don't skip this step)
Confectioners' sugar for topping

Whisk together all but the flour until well-combined. Sift flour over mixture and whisk thoroughly until no white lumps are showing. Pour lemon custard over prebaked shortbread, baking for an additional 25 minutes, until center is no longer jiggly. Cool completely. Sift confectioners' sugar over top. Cut into small squares. *Makes about 20 to 24 pieces.*

CITRUS CURD

I fell in love with citrus sometime in my forties, when my palate shifted and I started craving all kinds of flavors I wasn't particularly excited about before. (See Pasta Puttanesca, for another example.) It turns out that lemon curd is the perfect union of my midlife obsession with citrus and my lifetime love of custard. Like its quieter sibling, a "curd" is an English custard of sorts, but with a base of butter instead of milk. It gets its name from the fact that the butter mixed with lemon (or other citrus) juice takes on a curdled appearance, at least until the butter melts. Curd is a classic British dish dating to the nineteenth century, but it is has become popular in Mediterranean countries as well, where citrus fruits are plentiful.

The origin of citrus is murky, though these ancient fruits are traceable as far back as the Stone Age, which ended over five thousand years ago. The four original citrus species were citron, a lemon ancestor (known in Hebrew as an *etrog*); pomelo, a grapefruit predecessor; mandarin, from the orange family; and papeda, an ancestor of the lime. All other citrus varieties are said to have sprung from these four.

This dish is the very essence of creamy citrus intensity without any bitterness or gritty rind. I use two pieces of kitchen equipment for curd: first, I recommend a microplane to make the zest—a tiny grater that captures the flavorful rind without the bitter white pith underneath (if you don't have one, grate gently on smallest side of a conventional grater); second, I use a food processor to blend the zest with the sugar, as it binds the two together. This binding is crucial, allowing the sugar to absorb the citrus oils. It can also be done by hand, working the zest and sugar between your fingers slowly until they fuse together.

This recipe can be made with any combination of citrus fruits, as long as it contains a tart variety like lime, lemon, or grapefruit as its base. Curds can also be made from non-citrus fruits like passion fruit, mango, and pineapple (though, of course, these do not have rinds for zesting). I have had great fun experimenting with various citrus-blended curds like clementine, Meyer lemon, and lime, or Cara Cara orange and pineapple. All of the combinations are smashing, and the classic lemon curd is also marvelous.

The order of this recipe matters greatly, so I have numbered the steps.

2 Tbsp. fresh citrus zest of your choice
1 c. granulated raw sugar
6 Tbsp. unsalted butter, softened
Generous ½ c. fresh citrus juice (balance sweet/tart)
Generous pinch of salt
2 whole eggs plus 2 egg yolks

1. Wash citrus rind, and zest using a microplane, if possible, taking care to avoid the pith (white part).

2. Place zest in a food processor with the sugar, and blend together for 1 to 2 minutes until zest binds to sugar completely; if working by hand, rub sugar and zest together between fingers a bit at a time. Be patient, rubbing until citrus fragrance is quite strong and sugar is moist and colored by the zest.

3. Add butter to citrus sugar in food processor and whir for a few seconds (or mix well by hand).

4. Add fresh citrus juice to sugar mixture, again whirring or mixing briefly.

5. Sprinkle in salt, then add 2 eggs and 2 yolks, one at a time, whirring or whisking for a few seconds after each addition. (See Sublime Chocolate Mousse for instructions on how to easily separate eggs.) Mixture will look curdled.

6. Place in heavy-bottom saucepan on low heat, stirring constantly with a rubber spatula for about 15 to 20 minutes. Butter will melt first and then mixture will gradually thicken enough to coat a wooden spoon.

7. Remove curd from heat and pour into mason jars or glass serving bowls. Cover with plastic wrap or lid and refrigerate immediately.

Presto! Sweet sunshine in a jar. Fine to eat as soon as it's cool (3 hours) but best if it sets overnight. Very rich and intensely flavored, so serve in small portions with berries and freshly whipped cream. Can also be used as filling for French Macarons or Sunshine Birthday Cake. Will keep for several weeks in fridge. *Makes 6 to 8 small servings, or filling for one layer cake or around two dozen macarons.*

CRÈME CARAMEL (FLAN)

Much as I love all things chocolate—whether rich and dark or milky and smooth—my favorite dessert of all time does not contain any: it's a marvelous, silky caramel custard called crème caramel, more commonly known as flan. My adoration arises partly from childhood nostalgia, since it is very popular all over Western Europe, and I often used to order it for dessert on special occasions. But its pleasures have endured for me through these many decades, and really, who could fail to be delighted by the beauty of its design? A little mountain of vanilla egg custard is baked over a bed of caramel, chilled, then inverted just before serving. The caramel flows down the mountain in a golden waterfall and pools on the platter, impossible to resist.

The origins of flan are not clear, but it certainly dates to the Roman Empire, when chickens were first domesticated and the resulting glut of eggs led to an explosion of culinary creativity. Flan began as a savory dish, a sort of flat quiche, but rose to enormous popularity when honey was added to the recipe. To this day, it remains ubiquitous throughout Latin cuisines, though the preparation varies from country to country: in Mexico it is made with sweetened condensed milk; the Cuban recipes contain more eggs; Spain favors the use of evaporated milk in its recipes; in France, which frequently claims the dish as its own invention (and can certainly claim both of its names), the custard is thickened with flour, and often baked in a thin crust.

My own recipe is a simple one, achieved through trial and error to recreate what I remember from my childhood: it's thickened with just a little heavy cream added to the milk, sunny-colored from extra egg yolks, light on the sugar, heavy on the vanilla, and abundant with caramel.

A note about preparation time: This dish needs about 45 minutes to assemble, another 45 minutes to bake, and at least 4 hours to cool, so plan accordingly.

Before beginning, set aside a mid-sized, round casserole dish (1½ or 2 quarts) for the Crème Caramel. While it's true that flan (like its cousin, crème brûlée) is often served in individual ramekins, a single, mid-sized casserole dish works fine here and is a lot easier. You will also need a larger (9 x 13-inch) Pyrex or other baking pan for the water bath. Make sure the smaller dish fits inside the larger one; if it has handles, all the better—that will make it easier to remove from the hot water after it's baked.

CARAMEL
¾ c. raw or turbinado sugar
3 Tbsp. water

Place sugar and water in a small, heavy-bottom saucepan at medium-high heat. Bring to a boil, swirling pan a couple of times until sugar dissolves, about 2 to 3 minutes. Let mixture boil without stirring until it is a deep amber color, about 4 to 6 more minutes. Watch pan carefully the whole time (if the sugar burns, the caramel will likely be ruined and you will need to start again). When the bubbling mixture changes color and takes on a deep, golden brown hue, immediately remove from heat, swirl pan once to mix, and pour carefully into bottom of casserole dish. Whatever you do, *never touch hot caramel with your fingers*; because it is so sticky, it can cause deep burns. Set dish aside.

CUSTARD
2 c. whole milk
½ c. heavy cream
3 eggs plus 3 egg yolks
¼ tsp. salt
½ c. raw sugar
2 tsp. vanilla extract

Preheat oven to 350 degrees. Place milk and cream in a saucepan over medium heat, heating until milk is steaming and small bubbles appear around the edges (this is called *scalding*); do not allow to boil. While milk heats, whisk together the eggs, egg yolks, salt, and sugar in a separate bowl until light and frothy, about 1 minute. (See Sublime Chocolate Mousse, next, for instructions on how to separate eggs.)

Set a full kettle or saucepan of water to boil for water bath. Keep stirring milk so it doesn't burn!

When milk mixture is steaming, whisk in vanilla, then *very gradually* whisk hot milk into the egg mixture, taking breaks from pouring as needed so the eggs do not scramble, but continuing to whisk the whole time. (This is called *tempering*.) When the custard is well blended, hold a strainer over the casserole dish containing the caramel, and pour the custard through the strainer into the dish to catch any lumps.

Place larger, empty baking pan in oven, and gently set the casserole dish inside it. Carefully pour hot water from the kettle into the larger pan until it's halfway up the outside of the casserole dish. Try not to splash. Bake custard for about 45 minutes, until it is golden on top and appears set (it will still jiggle a bit but be firm to the touch). If you have doubts as to the custard's doneness, stick a butter knife into the center of the custard, halfway in (the cut won't show once you turn it upside down). The knife should come out just about clean; if it doesn't, bake for an additional 5 minutes. Try not to overbake it, or some small lumps might form in the custard; if that happens, it will still taste wonderful—it just won't be quite as smooth.

Slowly remove Crème Caramel from water bath, holding the edges of the casserole tightly with your oven mitts so it doesn't slip. Allow to cool on the counter for one hour. (Turn off oven so water bath can also cool before you empty it.) Move dish to fridge and chill for at least another 3 hours, and up to one day.

Unmold flan shortly before serving by running a thin, sharp knife slowly and completely around the side of the casserole. Invert a rimmed platter or a shallow bowl on top, hold both together tightly, and carefully flip them over. Set the bowl or platter down on the counter and lift the casserole to check that the flan has slid out; it should do so easily. Take care not to spill the caramel as it runs down the sides of the custard and onto the platter, creating a delicious golden lake.

Serve cold like a custard, spooning flan into individual dishes and topping with caramel sauce. Pass around a bowl of barely sweetened fresh whipped cream, if desired. *Makes about 6 to 8 servings.*

SUBLIME CHOCOLATE MOUSSE
AND CHOCOLATE MOUSSE MERINGUES

Like so many rich and commanding dishes in the Western culinary tradition, chocolate mousse originated in France. It first appeared in the mid-eighteenth century, and soon enough, whipped egg whites were being used to give a cloud-like lightness to a range of sweet and savory delicacies around the world, from salmon to raspberries. Chocolate mousse lends itself to all kinds of permutations: it can be used as a filling for cake or macarons (see French Macarons, next), layered with whipped cream and berries for a trifle, made with white chocolate for a creamy variation, or served on its own in a little parfait dish with some chocolate shaved on top. Mousse resembles its cousins, custard and pudding, in some respects, but it is frothy where they are smooth, and unlike either of them, mousse is stabilized by cold instead of heat.

Chocolate mousse is really quite easy to make, provided that you follow the directions exactly. It shouldn't take you more than twenty minutes to assemble, but there are a couple of crucial elements that make for a successful chocolate mousse, specifically, bringing the eggs to room temperature, and using high quality chocolate. (Since the egg whites need an hour to come to room temperature first, and the mousse does need several hours to set afterward, it's not quite a speedy process, when all is said and done.) Whatever you do, don't forget the salt! In this recipe, the salt particularly complements the depth and richness of the chocolate, adding contrast and complexity. I also add almond extract which ups the intensity of the chocolate flavor and tastes distinctly liquor-like in this context. Of course, it can be omitted in favor of vanilla if you prefer. But I think the almond flavor makes this mousse memorable.

A bonus fact about chocolate mousse is that it can be baked into meringue cookies, using the same recipe but omitting the whipped cream. When you bake mousse, the egg whites deconstruct in the heat, and you are left with flat, chewy, dark chocolate meringue cookies that beg to be eaten immediately (because they dry out easily and also because they are fabulous). More instructions for the meringues follow the directions for mousse.

SUBLIME CHOCOLATE MOUSSE

6 egg whites at room temperature
10 - 12 oz. quality bittersweet chocolate or chips
1½ tsp. almond extract
Scant ½ tsp. salt
½ c. raw fine sugar
1 pint heavy cream, whipped and divided
2 Tbsp. raw fine sugar
Fresh berries for serving, optional

Take eggs out of fridge and separate them at least one hour before beginning. If you forget, you can place them in a small deep bowl inside a larger bowl of warm—not hot—water to speed the process along.

3 easy steps to separate eggs:
1. Set two bowls side-by-side on the counter in front of you. Crack an egg against the counter's surface.

2. Hold cracked egg over left bowl. Split eggshell apart carefully with both thumbs,, dropping egg onto your clean, slightly cupped palm. Open fingers just enough to let the white slip through while keeping yolk in place. (If a spot of yolk gets into the whites, use a clean teaspoon to fish it out. If the yolk really breaks and a lot of it gets into the whites, I recommend you start over, as egg whites will not set.)

3. When all of egg white has slipped through your fingers, move cupped hand to the right bowl and drop the yolk in. Reserve yolks in fridge (try using them to make Citrus Curd or Vanilla Egg Custard). Repeat.

While egg whites are coming to room temperature, melt chocolate chips or broken chocolate bars in a glass bowl set over a small saucepan of water, or in the microwave. If using the stove top method, stir every couple of minutes until chocolate is melted and smooth. If using the microwave, the chocolate will heat unevenly, so begin with 1 minute and add 30 seconds at a time, stirring in between to avoid burning the chocolate. When smooth and nearly all melted, stir thoroughly and allow to cool. It is important that the chocolate is no longer hot when it's mixed with the beaten egg whites or they will deconstruct.

Pour egg whites into dry bowl of an electric mixer. Line up the rest of the ingredients within arm's reach and turn beaters to high speed. As soon as the whites turn frothy and start looking more white than clear, add almond extract and salt. Once the egg whites begin to form a visible structure, pour sugar in slowly, in a continuous stream with mixer still at high speed, continuing to beat until egg whites are stiff and glossy, about 2 to 3 more minutes. You will know they're done when they clump up on the beater and do not fall off after you've stopped it. With mixer off, slowly fold in melted and cooled chocolate with a rubber spatula until completely integrated. Mixture will collapse a bit and might look slightly liquidy, but that's okay. When the mousse gets cold, it will thicken up again. Transfer into a non-metallic bowl.

Whip heavy cream with 2 Tbsp. sugar in a clean, dry mixing bowl, and reserve half in the fridge for serving later. If using sweetened nondairy whip, do not add extra sugar when beating. (This recipe can be made without the whipped cream altogether, but the mousse will be extremely intense and dark. In that case, you might want to serve it in very small quantities or bake it into Chocolate Mousse Meringues, as below.)

Fold other half of whipped cream into mousse, using a rubber spatula and folding slowly until the two are fully integrated. The mousse will look surprisingly light now but will darken again as it sets. Some small bits of chocolate might have solidified in your mousse, but that's okay—they add lovely texture. Pour into a glass serving bowl or individual parfait cups, cover tightly, and place in fridge until set, at least 4 hours. Serve with more whipped cream and fresh berries. Stores well in fridge or freezer. *Serves 8 to 12*.

WHITE CHOCOLATE VARIATIONS
This recipe can also be made as white chocolate mousse using the same quantity of good-quality white chocolate (with cocoa butter as a primary ingredient) and the directions above. Or divide beaten egg whites before adding melted chocolate and make two batches for a dramatic black-and white presentation, or try baking the dark chocolate batch into meringues (below), and serve as a garnish on the white mousse.

CHOCOLATE MOUSSE MERINGUES
Preheat oven to 325 degrees. Make one batch chocolate mousse recipe (above), omitting whipped cream.

Using two cookie sheets lined with parchment paper, drop teaspoonfuls of mousse at least two inches apart, no more than 15 to a cookie sheet—they will spread quite a lot during baking.

Bake for 12 to 15 minutes, rotating pans halfway through. When meringues are shiny and flat, remove and allow to cool before peeling off parchment. Platter in a single layer so they don't stick together. Sublime as a garnish for white chocolate mousse or on their own with a strong cup of coffee. *Makes 30 to 35 cookies*.

FRENCH MACARONS

Is there anything more wonderful than a macaron? This is not to be confused with the humbler Passover "macaroon," which is a lot less delicate due to the addition of shredded coconut and other ingredients. A macaron is a confection of sugar, almond flour, and egg white that is whipped, allowed to rest, and baked at relatively low temperature. The result is a cookie that is light as air on the outside and delightfully chewy on the inside. It is traditionally sandwiched around a filling; some of my favorites include—but are by no means limited to—Citrus Curd, all kinds of buttercream, and sweetened mascarpone (see variations below), with a few drops of food coloring added for fun. Macarons are often made in whimsical colors, but making them is no laughing matter, as the process is subject to shifts of weather, mood, and destiny. Sometimes, they simply fail to come together. When they're right, they rock.

The word *macaron* comes from the Italian *maccherone,* meaning "fine dough." Though the French undoubtedly made them famous, macarons had their beginnings in Italy: it is believed that they were imported to France in 1533 by Catherine de' Medici upon her marriage to King Henry II. In our family, it was my son, Jesse, who first undertook this culinary adventure. This recipe, which he shared with me, has worked well, maybe because I followed the experts' recommendation to use a kitchen scale. You will see that I have given the weights of the ingredients first here, followed by the measurements, for those who don't have a kitchen scale. In that case, just measure very carefully, using a knife to level dry ingredients. You will also need a food processor and a pastry piping bag (or in a pinch, a freezer bag with the corner snipped). Macarons take a while to make: allow a good 4 hours from start to table, much of it time for the egg whites to rest at various stages. For your own sanity, avoid making these on a humid day. They are finicky and can easily defy your best efforts. But when your mood and the weather align, just go for it. Your wholeheartedness will be rewarded with sweet, chewy, light little bundles of wonder.

MACARON SHELL

120g room temperature egg whites (around 4 large egg whites)
200g confectioners' sugar (scant 2 c.)
100g almond flour (scant 1 c.)
1.25g salt (¼ tsp.)
40g sifted superfine granulated sugar or caster sugar (3 Tbsp.)
Desired flavoring and/or colors (suggestions below)

1. Separate eggs and bring whites to room temperature. (For instructions on how to separate eggs, see previous recipe for Sublime Chocolate Mousse.)

2. Using a kitchen scale for grams or a knife to level your cups, measure out and combine confectioners' sugar and almond flour in a food processor and pulse for 30 seconds until integrated and fine. Set aside.

3. In a completely dry, clean bowl, beat the egg whites and salt together on medium speed for 1 minute. Switch to high speed and beat just until stiff peaks form, about 2 more minutes. Beat in superfine sugar, 1 Tbsp. at a time for a total of 1 more minute. (If you don't have superfine sugar, grind granulated sugar in food processor for 20 to 30 seconds.) Do not overbeat. Mixture should be glossy and stiff but not dry.

4. On low speed, beat in any flavors or colors now, just until integrated. Here are some ideas:

For maple variation, use 2 drops yellow, 1 red to achieve golden tan color. Add ½ tsp. almond extract, ½ tsp. maple extract, ¼ tsp. Vietnamese cinnamon.

For citrus variation, use 3 drops yellow and 2 red for orange hue. Add ½ tsp. orange extract, 2 Tbsp. orange zest, blended in food processor with confectioners' sugar and almond flour (see step 1 above).

For raspberry variation, use 2 to 3 drops red coloring to get pink or red color. Add ½ tsp. vanilla extract.

5. Fold egg white mixture into almond flour mixture until well combined. Be very gentle and light-handed with rubber spatula but mix thoroughly. When done, the mixture will be smooth, sticky, and glossy. Let batter sit, uncovered, at room temperature for 20 minutes.

6. Fit piping bag with a piping tip, and line 2 cookie sheets with parchment paper. Do not preheat oven yet.

7. Fill piping bag with batter and pipe even-sized rounds onto baking sheets—hold the bag vertically and close to the baking sheet. While piping, the batter will spread out slightly, so keep that in mind. You want to end up with 2-inch circles, 1 to 2 inches apart. Pick baking sheets up and, holding them tightly, bang them down on the counter to get rid of any large air bubbles. Pop stubborn ones carefully with a toothpick. The air bubbles make the macarons crack, so you want as few as possible. If using any edible decorations (like cinnamon), sprinkle onto the wet round shells at this point. I leave them bare.

8. Let the piped rounds sit on the cookie sheets for at least 45 minutes and up to 1 hour. Set a timer. This is crucial to making macarons! The air will help the rounds set and form a dry shell. They should not be sticky going into the oven.

9. When this resting time is almost up, preheat oven to 325 degrees, on the convection setting if you have one. Test rounds for readiness by very gently touching a couple of them with your knuckle or fingertip. They should be dry enough not to leave any sticky residue.

10. Bake the macarons for 10 minutes, one baking sheet at a time. Rotate the pan at the 5-minute mark. When done, the tops should be crisp and risen above their signature crinkly base or "foot." Allow to cool completely on the baking sheet before assembling (see filling ideas below). Use caution when peeling them off the parchment paper; if the bottoms are at all sticky, use a thin metal spatula or knife to loosen them.

11. Put 1 tsp. or more filling (depending how thick you want it) on the flat side of half the shells and place the other half of the shells on top to form the iconic French macaron. Store in fridge, but bring to room temperature before serving. Leftover macarons can be covered and kept in the fridge for up to 3 days.

SIMPLE BUTTERCREAM
1 c. softened, unsalted butter (2 sticks)
2 c. confectioners' sugar, sifted
¼ tsp. salt
1 tsp. pure vanilla exract

Beat ingredients together until smooth and spreadable.

MAPLE MASCARPONE BUTTERCREAM

Add following ingredients to simple buttercream. (See macaron shell recipe for food coloring ideas.)

¼ c. mascarpone or whipped cream cheese
½ tsp. maple extract
¼ tsp. cinnamon (pref. Vietnamese)

SUNRISE CITRUS BUTTERCREAM

Add following ingredients to simple buttercream, but omit vanilla, and blend citrus zest with confectioners' sugar in food processor before adding other ingredients. (See macaron shell recipe for food coloring ideas.)

1 Tbsp. fresh lemon juice
2 Tbsp. orange or lemon zest
¼ c. mascarpone (or cream cheese)
½ tsp. orange extract

RASPBERRY MASCARPONE FILLING

Do not use buttercream. Blend all ingredients below until smooth. (See macaron shell recipe above for food coloring ideas.)

½ c. mascarpone or cream cheese
¼ c. seedless raspberry jam
1 stick (½ c.) unsalted butter
2 c. confectioners' sugar
¼ tsp. salt

Of course, there are a hundred variations to try, everything from using the simple buttercream to filling your macarons with Sublime Chocolate Mousse (previous recipe) or Citrus Curd. Let your whims be your guide. Have fun! And may the macaron goddess be with you. *Makes about 3 dozen filled macaron pairs.*

APRICOT MANDELBROT

There were apricot trees in the garden of my childhood home in Zurich, so I have a deep, nostalgic attachment to this fruit. I always loved their shape and color, the way they demanded to be treated with care, nestled softly in the palm of my hand. Every year, I am thrilled when they appear for their brief season; that lovely blush of pinkish red over the warm orange makes me think of sunset after a perfect summer day. So it will come as no surprise that apricots are the filling for my all-time favorite cookies.

Traditional mandelbrot are a lot like biscotti, in that they are baked in a log, sliced, and then baked again until they are hard and crumbly. It's not completely clear whether the origins of mandelbrot (literally "almond bread") lie with Italian biscotti, but however they began, they certainly became very popular among the Ashkenazi Jews of Eastern Europe and have endured as a treat through many generations.

As a fan of anything almond, I loved the *idea* of mandelbrot, but I found that the cookie itself was not so exciting. I was looking for a softer cookie, one I could enjoy even if I wasn't dunking it; I wanted a cookie with more depth of flavor—and more nutrients—than one made with just white flour.

This recipe is the result of all that over-thinking: once-baked mandelbrot made with almond flour as well as conventional flour, and a relatively small amount of sugar. They are the same shape as the traditional cookie, but their texture and taste are more like a cross between shortbread and apricot rugelach (another perennial Jewish favorite). They are soft, not super-sweet, and as a bonus, the almond flour increases the cookie's nutritional content by quite a bit. But of course, the main reason to make them is because they are delectable. Once you start eating these little beauties, it's hard to stop.

1½ c. unbleached all-purpose flour
½ c. blanched almond flour
1¼ tsp. baking powder
½ c. raw sugar
Scant 1 tsp. salt
½ c. vegetable or canola oil
2 eggs, lightly beaten
1½ tsp. pure almond extract
Approx. ½ c. apricot jam (not "fruit spread") for fillir

Preheat oven to 350 degrees. Mix all dry ingredients in a medium bowl. Make a well in the center and add oil, beaten eggs, and extract—the almond extract is crucial to this recipe, so don't skip it! (The salt is crucial here, too, as it usually is.) Mix dough until well combined; it will be oily and sticky, but you should be able to work with it. If it seems impossible, try adding a couple of tablespoons of extra flour.

Divide dough into 2 balls and place them side-by-side in the center of a greased nonstick cookie sheet. (The jam sometimes runs out of the middle and becomes extra sticky in the heat, so it's important to grease the pan even if you are starting with a good nonstick surface.) Use your palm to flatten and elongate each ball of dough, shaping with your fingers to create two rectangular strips that span the length of the cookie sheet, about a quarter- to a half-inch thick and about 4 inches wide. They should be fairly uniform in width and not touching each other. Place spoonfuls of jam on each strip, using back of spoon to spread a line evenly down the middle, leaving about an inch of dough all the way around.

With the tips of your fingers, gently loosen the edges of dough on each long side and fold toward the center over the jam, pressing down lightly, so only about a half-inch strip of filling is left visible in the middle. Sometimes the edges of the dough will crack or separate a bit; just use your fingers to gently press them back together, trying not to squeeze the jam out of the center. A few little cracks are fine. After dough has been folded from both long sides, fold short ends as well, pressing down lightly to smooth seams and seal edges.

Bake for about 30 to 35 minutes, until golden brown (watch out for burning). Remove from oven and allow to cool briefly, so cookies can harden slightly before you cut them. After less than five minutes, use a non-scratch spatula to cut each log into uniform strips of about 1 inch wide, so you end up with around 20 to 25 pieces total. Do not allow to cool all the way before cutting, as the loaf is more likely to crumble and the cookies to fall apart. Take care when cutting, as pieces can sometimes be weak and break in the middle where the jam is. But don't worry too much—broken pieces are fair game for nibbling.

You can easily substitute raspberry, blackberry, or any other flavor of jam, or try using ¼ c. chocolate chips or Nutella for one of the loaves. Note that with chocolate variations, cookies will be drier (since they won't get the moisture from the jam), so place on a separate pan and remove from oven a few minutes sooner.

If storing mandelbrot to serve later, cool completely first, and place layers of parchment or wax paper between the layers of cookies so they don't stick to each other. These store well in an airtight container for several days—if they last that long. *Makes about two dozen pieces.*

TARTE AUX POMMES (FRENCH APPLE TART)

Apples—I love them so! They bring a lovely crunch to Creamy Curried Chicken Salad, add juicy texture grated into my Muesli and Frogurt, taste perfect cooked into Curried Fruited Rice. My favorite afternoon snack? A crisp apple cut into wedges, with a hunk of Gouda and a handful of walnuts. Serena has always shared this passion for apples with me, and earlier this year, when we both decided to move back to Connecticut, we shared a moment of glee at the promise of all those New England apples. Now, as I write this, they are in their glory.

Fall also brings the Jewish High Holidays, which have long made use of this seasonal convergence: apples and honey are consumed at Rosh Hashanah to usher in a sweet new year and to symbolize the circularity of the year. Apple and honey cakes abound during this holiday, too, and they are wonderful—but I favor a French *tarte aux pommes* as the lighter dessert for these heavy, festive meals.

This recipe is a classic apple tart like you might find in just about any bakery in France. Unlike an American apple pie, it has a rich almond filling—called *frangipane* or almond cream—underneath a spiral layer of tightly arranged apples; instead of a second crust on top, it is brushed with apricot jam, giving it a sweet, golden sheen. In Europe, *frangipane* is used to fill all sorts of delightful treats. I hope you discover them all!

In the tradition of French cooking, this recipe takes a little while. Leave yourself a good hour for preparation, not including the extra hour to chill the tarte crust. The final effect is dramatic, and the fall flavors of tart apple contrasting with the rich, sweet *frangipane* is nothing short of brilliant.

TARTE CRUST
¼ c. raw almonds
¼ c. confectioners' sugar
¼ c. unbleached all-purpose flour
½ c. butter (or margarine), softened
1 egg yolk
1 tsp. almond extract
¼ tsp. salt

Use a 12-inch fluted tarte pan with a removable bottom. Grind together almonds and confectioners' sugar in food processor until the mixture looks like coarse sand. Add remaining ingredients and pulse until dough comes together and all components are integrated. Roll out dough with a rolling pin on parchment paper until smooth and flat enough to span the tarte pan, with extra for the sides. With dough on parchment, turn over on top of pan and press into pan evenly. Leave parchment in place and chill dough in refrigerator for at least 1 hour and up to 4, remembering to peel the paper off when ready to fill.

FRANGIPANE FILLING
2 c. blanched almond flour
½ tsp. salt
½ c. butter (or margarine), softened
½ c. raw sugar
2 eggs
1 tsp. pure almond extract
1 tsp. good quality vanilla extract
2 Tbsp. dark rum

Preheat oven to 375 degrees.

Mix almond flour and salt in a small bowl. In larger bowl, cream ½ c. butter or margarine and ½ c. sugar with an electric mixer until mixture is fluffy and sugar is dissolved. Beat in eggs, extracts, and rum; add almond flour mixture and beat until smooth. Spread frangipane into chilled tart shell. Set aside.

APPLE TOPPING

3 - 4 apples, cored, peeled, sliced thinly and uniformly*
2 Tbsp. butter (or margarine), softened
1 Tbsp. sugar
Lemon juice to prevent browning
6 oz. apricot jam, warmed and strained

*An apple peeler/corer/slicer (illustrated above) costs less than $20. (As far as I know, this little tool does not have a more elegant name.) If you are an apple lover, it will save you an untold number of hours over its lifetime (see also Potato Latkes and Applesauce). With this contraption, you will get perfectly circular apple rings that you simply need to cut in half for beautiful, uniform slices on your tarte. If you don't have one, just peel and core the apples as usual, and slice them as uniformly as possible into thin half-moons.

Peel, core, and slice apples, working as quickly as you safely can, and sprinkling slices with a little lemon juice as you work to prevent browning.

Returning to the tarte shell, arrange apple slices in tightly overlapping spirals on top of frangipane, from the outside to the middle of the tart, choosing larger slices for the outside circle, and smaller ones as the circle tightens; be as artful as possible. Dot apples with 2 Tbsp. butter or margarine, and sprinkle with 1 Tbsp. sugar.

Bake tarte for 50 to 60 minutes until golden, checking to be sure crust is not burning. (If it is looking ominously dark, crimp foil carefully around edges and turn oven down to 350.) Remove from oven when apples have softened and almond cream has puffed up around them.

Gently warm apricot jam (30 seconds in microwave or a couple of minutes on the stove). Push warm jam through a strainer to remove any lumps, and use a pastry brush to apply to the surface of the tart until it is shiny and golden. Allow to cool for at least 30 minutes before serving.

I recommend serving with a really good vanilla ice cream, and a dessert wine like a *Spätlese* (late Riesling), or a dark cup of Earl Grey tea. *Makes about 6 to 8 servings.*

JESSE'S TARTE TATIN

Tarte Tatin was created in the 1880s by two French sisters, Stéphanie and Caroline Tatin, at their hotel outside Paris—and it has since become one of France's most iconic desserts. It is an upside-down caramel apple tart that begins in a skillet, where the apples turn golden as they caramelize with butter and sugar. A circle of puff pastry is placed on top just before the pan goes into the oven, and the whole thing is flipped over to serve. Puff pastry, or in French, *pâte feuilletée*, is a delicate, flaky dough that can be found in most grocery freezer sections (that is where I get mine). This is one of Jesse's favorite recipes from his time in culinary school. The ingredients are stunningly simple, but the result is a veritable stealth-bomb of flavor.

4 Tbsp. unsalted butter, softened
Approx. 1-lb. box frozen puff pastry
Pinch of salt
4 Granny Smith or other tart apples
4 Tbsp. superfine sugar, pref. raw

An hour before you begin, remove butter from fridge and puff pastry from freezer. You will need a heavy, nonstick 8-inch sauté pan with an oven-safe handle. When pastry is defrosted, unroll and press out an 8-inch circle of dough (a round cake pan works well). Cover and set aside. Peel, core, and quarter apples.

Preheat oven to 400 degrees. Spread soft butter in sauté pan. Add pinch of salt and sprinkle superfine sugar over butter. Place pan on stove over medium heat, stirring gently until combined. After butter melts, mixture will bubble and start to turn golden, about 5 to 7 minutes. Watch very carefully that caramel doesn't turn too dark or burn. It should be light brown but not thick yet. Remove from heat.

Being *very careful* not to let your fingers touch hot caramel, place apple quarters on their sides in pan, leaning them against each other in a tight circle, crowding them in so they keep their position when they begin to cook down. Return pan to medium heat and cook until apples begin to soften and caramel bubbles up around them, about 10 to 15 minutes. Remove from stove and place puff pastry circle on top of apples. Place pan immediately in oven, and bake until pastry is golden and puffy, 25 to 30 minutes.

Remove pan from oven. Slide a rubber spatula carefully under apples to loosen. Hold a platter tightly over pan and flip, inverting tarte carefully onto serving plate. Serve warm. *Makes about 4 to 6 servings.*

BAKED APPLES WITH WALNUTS, YELLOW RAISINS, AND BROWN SUGAR

When I was in middle school, we lived on a road that ran alongside a large apple orchard, and sometimes in the fall, I would walk home from school instead of taking the bus, just so I could stop and pick the apples when the trees were heavy with them. They were crisp and tart, their skins warm from the still-high sun. I fell in love with apples then, and to this day, the promise of fall's apple bounty—along with the blazing colors of the leaves—gives me solace when summer is waning.

But the seasons must change, and eventually, the apples must soften. That's when this recipe comes in. While it is very simple, it is unfailingly delicious, the perfect ending to a heavy meal on a winter's evening. I've been making it for years, and it never comes out quite the same, but it never disappoints, either.

6 large baking apples (like Fuji or Braeburn)
¼ c. dried California apricots
6 Tbsp. brown sugar
3 Tbsp. salted butter, softened
1 tsp. cinnamon
¼ c. yellow raisins
½ c. chopped walnuts
½ to ¾ c. boiling water

Preheat oven to 350 degrees. Use a paring knife or apple corer to remove stems and seeds from apples, making a hole from end to end for filling, but leaving fruit intact. Stand apples in a large, deep baking dish.

Snip apricots into small pieces. Place brown sugar, 2 Tbsp. butter, raisins, apricots, and cinnamon in a bowl and mix well to combine. Add nuts. Stuff mixture into apples and dot with remaining Tbsp. butter. Pour boiling water around apples and place carefully in oven. (For an extra kick, add ¼ cup rum.)

Bake for 30 to 45 minutes, until the apples are cooked through and tender (can easily be pierced with a fork) but not mushy. Remove from the oven and baste with the juices from the pan. Serve warm, with good vanilla ice cream and the juices spooned over the top. *Makes 6 servings.*

BLUEBERRY CRUMBLE

This recipe is a bona fide family favorite. I've been making it since before I became a mother; now my oldest, Gabriella, is a mother herself, and she requested it especially for this cookbook. Blueberries grow in abundance in North America—and many other parts of the world—exploding into sweet profusion in late summer and early fall. Blueberry season always reminds me of the children's books *Jamberry* and *Blueberries for Sal*, stories that celebrate the joys of this ancient fruit, and that I associate with the memory of reading aloud to my own children, nestled drowsily in my lap. I loved those baby days, and I am overjoyed to be reliving them now with my grandson, Asher.

Use fresh, seasonal blueberries that have gone a bit soft, or make it in winter with frozen wild blueberries.

3 c. fresh or frozen blueberries
Juice of 1 whole lemon
2 Tbsp. raw granulated sugar
2 c. rolled oats (not instant)
½ c. butter, softened, plus more for top
¾ c. brown sugar
1 tsp. cinnamon
½ tsp. salt
½ c. chopped walnuts (optional)

Preheat oven to 350 degrees. Toss blueberries with lemon juice and raw sugar, and spread in a mid-sized glass or ceramic dish. Mix remaining ingredients together by hand in a large bowl to create streusel topping, making sure butter, brown sugar, and cinnamon really coat oats and nuts (if using) until it's the consistency of damp dirt. Spread streusel mixture evenly over the fruit. Dot with butter. Bake for 45 to 60 minutes until fruit is bubbling and topping is brown and toasty. Best served warm for breakfast, or with vanilla ice cream for dessert—or with vanilla ice cream for breakfast. Who's going to argue? No matter what, I hope you take some time yourself to sit down and enjoy the jammy, warm fruit and buttery streusel topping.

This dish can also be made with apples, peaches, or any other fruit that lends itself to baking. Just be sure it's bubbling around the edges before you remove it from the oven. *Makes about 6 to 8 servings.*

GRILLED PINEAPPLE WITH CINNAMON CRÈME FRAICHE

It was celebrity chef Bobby Flay who first introduced me to grilled fruit—and what a revelation! Both the concept and the man. I had been watching his show, *Boy Meets Grill*, for some time already when Jesse and I had the chance to meet him, and we found that he was even more dynamic in person than on screen. He was brimming with energy and ideas, and this one really made an impression on me. When fruit is grilled, it turns smoky and dark, rendering its sugars in the high heat and caramelizing gorgeously. Pineapple is my personal favorite for grilling, but see my note below for alternatives.

This is an especially easy dish to make when you are already grilling something for dinner (see Garlic Lemon Chicken Breasts or Rib Eye Steak Chimichurri—another Bobby Flay favorite), so you won't be heating up the grill just to make dessert. That said, if you will be grilling meat at the same time, be sure to preheat and scrape the grill before you start, and grill the fruit first so it doesn't end up tasting like meat.

A drizzle of crème fraiche—French sour cream—mixed with cinnamon and honey makes this simple dish elegant and satisfying, especially if you are able to serve the fruit warm or reheat it before serving, to get that blissful contrast between the warm, smoky fruit and the cool crème fraiche. *Makes about 6 to 8 servings.*

GRILLED PINEAPPLE
1 ripe pineapple, cut into short planks (as below)
2 Tbsp. extra virgin olive oil or more if needed
1 tsp. honey or agave if pineapple is not super sweet

Using a sharp knife, cut top and bottom off pineapple as evenly as possible, so it can be stood up straight. Cut downward to remove rind in five or six large strips, trying not to dig into the fruit too much (and being very careful of your fingers). You will now have a pentagonal or hexagonal fruit, but you still need to remove the hard circular core. Cut each flat side of the pineapple off in a long, thick plank, as close to the core as possible but taking care not to include it. Lay the planks down on their flat sides and cut each one the short way into smaller planks, about 1 to 2 inches thick. You should end up with around 3 dozen pieces that are wide enough to set across a grill without falling through.

With a pastry brush, coat the pineapple planks with olive oil on both sides. Set planks diagonally across a preheated grill or grill pan on medium-high for 2-4 minutes per side. Grill marks should be golden brown and the fruit should begin to soften. Do not blacken fruit (pineapples have a lot of sugar, so they burn easily). Remove from heat and drizzle with agave if the pineapple is a bit tart. Cover to keep warm.

CINNAMON CRÈME FRAICHE
8-oz. container crème fraiche (or sour cream)
½ tsp. Vietnamese cinnamon
1 - 2 Tbsp. honey, to taste
1 - 2 Tbsp. milk or cream

Whisk together first three ingredients, then add just enough milk or cream to make the crème fraiche easy to drizzle. Serve grilled fruit warm with a flourish of cinnamon crème fraiche over each plate.

STONE FRUIT VARIATIONS
This dish can also be made with any ripe but firm stone fruit: about 6 to 10 plums, peaches, apricots, or nectarines, depending on size. Choose whatever looks best to you. Cut each fruit in half as evenly as possible, remove pits, brush flat sides with olive oil and place face-down on the grill for 2-4 minutes. If fruits are large, you can cut into quarters and grill on two sides, watching the time. After fruit is removed from grill, taste for sweetness, and if it is tart, drizzle with tiny amounts of agave while still hot. Serve face up so grill marks show, laced with cinnamon crème fraiche.

CHOCOLATE BIRTHDAY CAKE WITH BUTTERCREAM FROSTING

When I was young, my father used to give us presents on his own birthday, as if to say in his quiet way that he was glad to be alive and wanted to share his good fortune with those he loved. Perhaps this is why birthdays have always been important to me. When my kids were growing up, I started a tradition of birthday breakfasts so I could begin showering them with gifts first thing in the morning. We upheld this tradition even if the big day fell during the school week; everyone just knew they had to get up fifteen minutes earlier than the usual ungodly hour. The incentive? Birthday cake for breakfast!

This classic chocolate layer with its easy one-bowl recipe has been the primary birthday cake in our family for decades, with variations on the buttercream that have included almond extract, espresso powder, peppermint extract (garnished with crushed red-and-white mint candies), raspberry cream (with mascarpone and seedless jam), and the old but never tired standby, vanilla. Baking a homemade birthday cake for those you love is not difficult, and it imparts such joy! This one only needs about 25 minutes to bake into a moist, dark chocolate cake that sticks to the fork, the plate, and wherever else it lands. Happy birthday to us all.

CAKE

1½ c. raw sugar
1¾ c. unbleached all-purpose flour
¾ c. cocoa powder
1½ tsp. baking powder
1½ tsp. baking soda
1 tsp. salt
2 eggs, lightly beaten
1 c. milk (or nondairy substitute)
½ c. vegetable/canola oil
2 tsp. vanilla extract
1 c. boiling water

Preheat oven to 350 degrees. Grease and flour two 9-inch round baking pans. Stir together sugar, flour, cocoa, baking powder, baking soda and salt in large bowl. Add eggs, milk, oil and vanilla; beat with electric mixer on medium speed for 2 minutes. Carefully stir in boiling water (batter will be quite thin). Pour into prepared pans. Bake cakes for 22 to 27 minutes, until tester inserted in center comes out with moist crumb still sticking to it (but no raw batter). Do not overbake. Cool completely before removing from pan.

BUTTERCREAM FROSTING

3 c. confectioners' sugar
1 c. unsalted butter (or margarine), softened
1 tsp. vanilla extract (or peppermint, orange, etc.)
1 tsp. almond extract (or additional tsp. alt. flavor)
¼ to ½ tsp. salt to taste
1 - 2 Tbsp. water or cream, as needed

With electric mixer, cream together confectioners' sugar, butter, extracts, and ¼ tsp. salt, beginning on low speed and increasing as sugar and butter integrate. When mixer is on high, add water or cream 1 tsp. at a time to reach desired texture: creamy and pliable but not runny. Taste and stir in more salt if needed. Use a third of frosting to cover first layer, stack second layer on top, and cover top and sides with remaining buttercream, swirling prettily and decorating liberally. Birthdays are the best! *Makes about 10 to 12 servings.*

ORANGE VELVET CAKE

Among my four kids, Serena has always had the most particular palate and palette—resulting in some unconventional food choices and an unbeatable artist's eye (she is the illustrator of this cookbook). While it's true that an orange Bundt cake is not your typical birthday fare, she has stuck by her favorite for over two decades. The crumb here is a bit dense, like an orange pound cake, so it benefits greatly from a bright, playful icing. Serena, who will soon be twenty-six, approaches her fluorescent orange-lemon icing with the same glee year after year. It took me a few birthdays to get it just right, but I have long since settled on an easy way to make different shades of orange that can be drizzled in layers, creating a celebratory confetti-like glaze. The icing hardens as it dries, leaving bright, shiny drips that are perfect for nibbling!

CAKE
1 c. raw or turbinado sugar
Zest of 1 large orange
2½ c. unbleached all-purpose flour
¾ tsp. salt
¾ tsp. baking soda
¾ c. butter (or margarine), softened
¾ c. orange juice
1 tsp. pure orange extract
1½ tsp. baking powder
3 eggs, beaten

Preheat oven to 350 degrees. Grease and lightly flour a Bundt pan and set aside.

Place sugar and orange zest in bowl of a food processor and blend for 1 to 2 minutes, or rub between fingers until sugar turns orange and zest is totally integrated.

Combine orange sugar with flour, salt, and baking soda in large mixing bowl. Add butter, orange juice, and orange extract. Beat with electric mixer on low for 2 minutes. Stir in baking powder, then add eggs and beat for 2 minutes. Pour batter into Bundt pan and bake at center of oven for 35 to 40 minutes, removing when cake is solid throughout, but moist crumbs cling to cake tester. Do not overbake.

Allow cake to cool completely before loosening sides with a rubber spatula and inverting onto a platter. Give the pan a gentle shake, and if the cake doesn't drop out, turn right-side-up and loosen again as needed with rubber spatula. Turn over again and gently unmold. Decorate with orange-lemon icing.

ORANGE-LEMON ICING
3½ c. confectioners' sugar
Generous pinch of salt
1 tsp. orange extract
¼ c. lemon juice
Red and yellow food coloring, if desired

Begin with 2 c. confectioners' sugar, pinch of salt, extract, and half of juice. Whisk until completely smooth. Add remaining sugar and juice alternately, just a little at a time, whisking between additions until you have a thick but still fluid icing. You should be able to pour it slowly, and it should be opaque, not translucent. Whisk in food coloring last (if desired), making it pale orange (5 yellow to 2 red drops) to begin. Pour half of icing over cake and smooth around sides with rubber spatula. Allow time for icing to set (it gets shiny and hard), then add 2 to 3 more drops of red to remainder of icing for brighter color, stirring well before dripping over cake in a crisscross or whirly pattern. If still more icing remains, add 1 or 2 drops yellow, stir, and drip over cake again. Have fun! Allow layers of icing to dry and harden completely before serving. *Makes about 10 to 12 servings.*

SUNSHINE BIRTHDAY CAKE WITH LEMON BUTTERCREAM (RACHEL'S 50TH BIRTHDAY CAKE)

When I was turning fifty, I realized that I was always making birthday cakes, but couldn't recall the last time I had received one. So, my sister Sonia and my friend Jeremy offered to make me one. I found that I did not crave the traditional chocolate birthday cake I usually make. What I wanted—what I was obsessed with—was citrus, with which I have been carrying on a midlife love affair. (See Citrus Curd for more about these ancient fruits.) In the long, dark months before my birthday at the end of March, I dream of the Italian lemon groves where sunshine grows on trees. Here, it is wrapped up in a bright and easy layer cake.

SUNSHINE CAKE
Zest and juice of 2 lemons or Myer lemons
1½ c. raw sugar
3 c. unbleached all-purpose flour
4 tsp. baking powder
Scant 1 tsp. salt
1 c. unsalted butter, softened (or margarine)
½ c. fresh-squeezed orange or clementine juice
1 c. whole milk (or substitute)
2 tsp. lemon extract
3 eggs, lightly beaten

Preheat oven to 350 degrees. Grease two 8- or 9-inch nonstick cake pans and set aside. Zest lemons and place zest with sugar in bowl of a food processor 1 to 2 minutes or blend with fingers until sugar is yellow and zest is integrated. Combine lemon sugar with flour, baking powder, and salt in mixing bowl. Juice lemons and add to dry mixture along with butter. Beat with electric mixer on medium for 2 minutes. Add orange juice, milk, lemon extract, and eggs, beating on medium for 2 more minutes until light and smooth.

Pour batter into cake pans and place on center rack of oven. Bake for 22 to 28 minutes, checking often after the 22-minute mark so you don't overbake. When tester comes out with moist crumbs still clinging (but no wet batter), remove from oven. Allow to cool completely before frosting.

LEMON BUTTERCREAM

Zest and juice of 1 - 2 lemons, more as needed
1 c. butter, softened
3 c. confectioners' sugar
½ tsp. salt
2 tsp. lemon extract
1 or 2 drops yellow food coloring, if desired

Zest lemons and add zest with confectioners' sugar to bowl of a food processor. Blend for 1 to 2 minutes until zest binds to sugar. Combine lemon sugar with softened butter, salt, and lemon extract, and cream together with electric mixer. Add half of lemon juice and beat for 1 minute until smooth and thick, then add remaining lemon juice 1 teaspoon at a time, beating between additions until desired consistency is reached (creamy but stiff enough to hold its own between layers). Add single drops of yellow food coloring if desired, blending to a lovely shade of sunshine. Turn one cake layer upside down on a platter and frost with one-third of buttercream. (Can also be filled with Citrus Curd). Place second cake layer right-side-up on top, and frost top and sides with remaining frosting. Decorate cheerily. *Serves 10 to 12.*

RASPBERRY SOUR CREAM BUNDT CAKE WITH KEY LIME ICING (ASHER'S WELCOME-TO-THE-WORLD CAKE)

This cake came into the world hot on the heels of my first grandson, Asher Meir. (See Poppi's Mushroom Barley Soup and Louis's New Father Soup for more about how he got his first and middle names.) The recipe reflects the festive spirit that accompanied his birth, with its bright, tangy icing and the fun swirl of intense raspberry in the middle, its pound-cake-like density lightened by the fruit flavors to a happy balance. I must have been quite thoroughly sleep-deprived when I started playing with this recipe, but somehow it did what I needed it to do, and bolstered us all for the next round of sleepless nights. Now that Asher is almost two years old and I know him a lot better, I am pleased to say that I chose well, as this cake is truly emblematic of his personality: playful and intense, tangy and sweet, with a core of gravitas, and no straight lines anywhere in sight. Asher, this one is most definitely for you.

3 c. unbleached all-purpose flour
1 tsp. baking powder
1 tsp. salt
1½ c. unsalted butter, softened
1½ c. raw or turbinado sugar
6 large eggs, room temperature
1 c. full-fat sour cream
2 tsp. vanilla extract
1 tsp. almond extract
½ c. seedless raspberry jam
½ c. fresh raspberries

Preheat oven to 350 degrees. Butter a high-quality nonstick Bundt pan.

Combine flour, baking powder, and salt in a small bowl. Set aside. With an electric mixer, beat butter and sugar together on high speed until creamy, scraping the bowl with a rubber spatula halfway through. Turn mixer to medium-high speed and add eggs one at a time, beating after each addition; then add sour cream and extracts. Turn mixer to low and add flour mixture, beating until just smooth and incorporated.

Transfer one-third of batter to a small bowl and add raspberry jam and raspberries. Batter will turn pink. Put half of remaining plain batter in Bundt pan. Add raspberry batter, then the rest of the plain batter on top. Use a knife to swirl the layers together. Don't over-swirl or the whole cake will be pink! Bake for 60 to 70 minutes, checking every few minutes from the 60-minute mark. Cake is done when tester comes out with a moist crumb but with no smudges of raw batter. The denseness of the pound cake can make the tester look clean even when the cake is not properly cooked. It's an easy mistake. I once brought this cake to a party while it was still raw in the middle! So check carefully, looking for the opaque "crumb" even if you have to pick at the surface of the cake a bit to be sure it's at that stage. Remember, the top of the cake will be the bottom, so a little divot or two won't show.

Allow cake to cool completely to room temperature before inverting onto cake plate to ice.

KEY LIME ICING
3 c. confectioners' sugar, sifted
Pinch of salt
2 - 4 Tbsp. fresh lime juice (pref. from key limes)
1 Tbsp. seedless raspberry jam, if desired

Whisk together sugar, pinch of salt, 2 Tbsp. lime juice (Nellie & Joe's Famous Key West Lime Juice® is a good substitute for fresh, if needed), and raspberry jam if you desire a pale pink hue. Whisk in more lime juice, 1 tsp. at a time, until icing is smooth and fluid; it should run off the whisk in a thick stream. Drizzle over cooled Bundt cake in whatever pattern you wish; layered shades of pink and white icing look especially lovely, and can be made by dividing icing before adding jam. Allow to harden for at least an hour and preferably overnight. Serve with a ring of fresh raspberries, if desired. *Makes about 10 to 12 servings.*

LINZER TORTE

I have been eating Linzer Torte since I was a child. It is a popular dessert in Germanic countries, and was always one of my favorites with its unique fragrance and flavors of almonds, cinnamon, and raspberries. I rediscovered it as an adult when I was looking for Passover desserts (it relies heavily on almonds for its base, so substituting matzah cake meal for the relatively small amount of flour was an easy modification), and my kids quickly came to love it, too. This torte takes some time to make, but it's well worth the effort.

Recently, I spent some time in the town of Linz, Austria, the place for which the Linzer Torte was named. This cake has been traced back to 1696—it is one of the world's oldest known cake recipes! But when I tried some at an ancient bakery there that claimed (along with several others) to be the originator of the Linzer Torte, it didn't taste the way I expected: it contained notes of citrus and nutmeg that were new to me. I realized that, like all recipes that have been around for hundreds of years, this one would have changed depending on where and when it was made. No one alive today can know what the original actually tasted like, but sense memories from childhood are a powerful force, so I have developed a recipe that is faithful to the Linzer Torte I remember.

Note: This torte is best when made at least 24 hours before serving. The flavors deepen overnight and reveal their full intensity. If serving the same day, it should be made as early in the morning as possible.

1½ c. whole almonds, toasted
¾ c. raw or turbinado sugar
1 tsp. cinnamon (pref. Vietnamese)
1½ c. unbleached all-purpose flour
½ tsp. salt
1 tsp. baking powder
1 c. butter (or margarine), softened
2 eggs, beaten lightly
2 Tbsp. rum or good vanilla extract
1 jar seedless raspberry jam (not low-sugar)

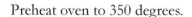

Preheat oven to 350 degrees.

Place almonds on a baking sheet in oven for ten minutes to toast; this deepens the flavor of the nuts dramatically. Do not over-toast or burn the almonds or they will become bitter. (If that happens, I recommend starting over. I know almonds are expensive but it would be unfortunate to go to all that trouble for a bitter aftertaste.)

Remove almonds from oven and allow to cool. Place in a food processor with ½ c. sugar and pulse to a powder. Be sure not to let the food processor go so long that the almonds turn to paste. This could affect the texture of the torte.

Add the remaining sugar, cinnamon, flour, salt, and baking powder, and pulse together until combined. Add the softened butter and pulse again until the dough looks like clumps of damp dirt. Add the eggs and rum or vanilla, and pulse until dough comes together into a smooth whole. Scrape dough carefully out of bowl and divide into two-thirds and one-third.

Place one-third of dough on a sheet of plastic wrap, lay more plastic wrap on top, and roll out with a rolling pin into approximately a 9-inch round. Freeze for 10 minutes. Take the remaining two-third of dough and press evenly into bottom and sides of a 9-inch springform pan. Make sure the dough comes up all the way around the sides.

Spread dough with raspberry jam, leaving a quarter-inch rim around the edge.

Remove smaller disc of dough from freezer, take off plastic wrap, and cut into 12 one-inch strips. Place 6 strips across raspberry jam going in one direction, then rotate the pan a half-turn and place the other 6 strips diagonally across the first 6, creating a lattice. Use your fingers to repair any broken strips and to press the ends of the dough gently into the bottom layer of dough so they are joined over the jam.

Bake in center of oven until top is golden brown and set, about 30 to 40 minutes. Do not overbake as cake will easily become dry—rather err on the side of underbaking. Cool completely before covering, and allow to rest for 24 hours before serving. Linzer Torte is heavenly with good vanilla ice cream or cinnamon gelato, but also stands very happily on its own, with just a fork and a cup of tea. *Makes about 8 to 10 servings.*

PECAN PIE

Pecans are the only tree nut native to North America, and the word *pecan* comes from a Native American word of Algonquin origins that was used to describe "all nuts requiring a stone to crack." Pecans grew wild for centuries in the river valleys of Mexico and throughout central and eastern North America; then, beginning in the seventeenth century, they were cultivated in the United States, gradually spreading southward and eventually becoming an enormous domestic and export industry in New Orleans and other port cities of the American south. The first recipes for pecan pie appeared during the nineteenth century in Texas, and it became wildly popular in the 1920s when a label recipe was printed on a bottle of Karo corn syrup. These sorts of stories are repeated throughout the cooking world, a reminder of the ways that commerce intersects with folk traditions to drive our food culture.

As in many American households, pecan pie has become a staple at our Thanksgiving table; the holiday itself has taken on an altered significance in this age of historical re-examination and soul-searching, and this is a crucial process we all must undertake—but our love for these familiar foods remains steadfast. (See Whole Berry Cranberry Sauce, Honey Cornbread, and Challah Stuffing for more Thanksgiving holiday thoughts and recipes.)

Pecan pie is like a toffee pudding with nuts swimming prettily in a lake of caramelized sugar. As they bake, the pecans float to the surface and arrange themselves in a lovely pattern on top of the caramelized custard, with no help at all. The salt here is critical for creating contrast with the caramel sweetness, and for the same reason, this pie is desperate for fresh whipped cream. When you take that first bite, close your eyes for a moment, and taste the pecan's journey unwinding through the sweet layers of flavor. *Serves 6 to 8.*

SIMPLE PIE CRUST

1 c. unbleached all-purpose flour
¼ tsp. salt
4 Tbsp. cold butter (or substitute)
3 Tbsp. cold water

This pie crust recipe is from my friend Jeremy, a dedicated pie maker.

Set aside a 9-inch pie pan. In a bowl, combine flour and salt. Cut butter into chunks and add, working with your hands to thoroughly integrate mixture so it looks like damp dirt. Gradually mix in cold water, up to 3 Tbsp., just until dough holds together but is not sticky; it will change consistency quickly. Form dough into a ball, place on a floured surface and use a rolling pin (or wine bottle) to roll the ball out into a circle just larger than your pie pan. Gently lift circle and lay it over the pan, pressing down so crust settles on bottom. Crimp dough around top edge of pan and trim excess with a butter knife. Set aside.

PECAN FILLING

1 c. corn syrup
3 eggs
2 Tbsp. butter (or margarine), melted
1 c. raw or turbinado sugar
½ tsp. salt
1 tsp. vanilla extract
1½ c. pecan halves, very fresh

Preheat oven to 350 degrees. Whisk together corn syrup and eggs. Melt butter and add to egg mixture. Pour in sugar and stir until combined. Stir in salt and vanilla and blend well. Add pecans and stir again to combine. Pour into pie crust and place carefully in center of oven on a cookie sheet. Bake for one hour, checking to be sure crust is not over-browning. If this occurs, cover edges with foil. Pie is done when it is the color of dark caramel and center springs back when tapped. Cool completely before covering.

Just before serving, whip a **pint of heavy cream** on high, adding **1 to 2 Tbsp. sugar** while beating. Pecan pie is best served at room temperature or very gently warmed, topped with fresh whipped cream.

MILK AND HARMONY PIE

David and I were both active musicians when we met—as were my parents, who started out performing for two neighboring Hadassah groups. With that kind of legacy, we made sure our children's lives were infused with our love of music. As they were growing up, we made four CDs of original Jewish and folk songs, one in honor of each of their bar/bat mitzvahs; our family "band" was called Milk and Harmony, and the kids contributed increasingly to these albums as their voices and musical personalities emerged. These days, they all make their own music out in the world. Jake is a professional guitarist and songwriter, fierce in his dedication and indisputable in his talent. Gabriella and Louis, who met in an a capella group at college, have carried on the family tradition with their own album of original Jewish and folk music. Jesse, who spent years organizing music festivals, has a tenor as sweet as this pie and a tremolo to take your breath away; and Serena's chocolaty voice knocks our socks off whenever she performs.

I've named this pie in honor of our family band, a variation on the "land flowing with milk and honey" from the Torah and an ever-poignant image as we all continue to seek our place to call home. Honey was also a particular favorite of my parents; every morning for as long as I can remember, they had it for breakfast with warm bread and butter. Whenever I cook with it, I think of their quiet mornings together.

So, what is this pie? It is a smooth, baked custard with a texture like pumpkin pie—a showcase for fresh cream and good honey that benefits from a sprinkle of salt at the end for that all-important contrast.

The preparation of the pie itself is not time-consuming, but it needs almost an hour to bake, and another hour to cool before you anoint it with salt.

Preheat oven to 350 degrees. Make one recipe Simple Pie Crust (see previous recipe for Pecan Pie), or in a pinch, use a premade pie crust. With a fork, gently poke several holes in the dough, and prebake for about 20 minutes. Remove from oven and allow to cool while preparing filling.

PIE FILLING

½ c. butter, melted
¼ c. raw sugar, plus 1 - 2 Tbsp. for whipped cream
2 Tbsp. fine white cornmeal or whole wheat pastry flour
¼ tsp. salt
¾ c. honey, pref. raw
1 tsp. cider vinegar
1 tsp. vanilla extract (like Madagascar or Bourbon)
3 eggs, lightly beaten
1½ c. heavy cream, divided
A good pinch of flaked sea salt to finish

All of the mixing for this pie can be done with a hand whisk and a rubber spatula.

Melt butter and combine with the ¼ cup sugar, cornmeal or wheat flour, and salt to make a paste. Add the honey, vinegar, and vanilla, and mix together. Fold in eggs, add ½ cup cream, and whisk together to blend.

Pour filling into prebaked pie shell and bake for 45 to 60 minutes. The filling will puff up like a marshmallow and the center will be just slightly wobbly, but it will settle. Set aside and allow to cool for an hour. Whip remaining 1 cup cream, adding 1 to 2 Tbsp. sugar early on so it has time to integrate before cream thickens. Whipped cream should not be very sweet; it is needed as a foil for the sweetness of the pie. Place in fridge until ready to serve. Once pie is cool to the touch, evenly sprinkle flaked salt on top. Serve at room temperature or cool, in small slices, with freshly whipped cream. Store in refrigerator. *Serves about 6 to 8.*

MEXICAN HOT CHOCOLATE BROWNIES

Mexican chocolate, with its base of ground cacao nibs, cinnamon, and sugar, is unique for both its flavor and texture; it is grainy and coarse, somewhat weightier than its distant cousins from Switzerland, Belgium, and France, and several thousand years older. The cacao tree is native to Mexico, and cocoa was cultivated by indigenous Mesoamerican populations such as the Aztecs, Olmecs, Mayans, Toltecs, Izapan, and Incas. Cacao was considered sacred, a pathway to the divine. It was a food (or more often, a drink) long before it became a candy—hence, its use in savory recipes like *mole*, a dark, rich sauce for meat and chicken.

These brownies are an homage to the age-old culinary traditions of Mexico, a country I have not yet had the opportunity to visit, but whose authentic flavors are among my favorites: cumin, oregano, and lime; cinnamon and cacao; chilies and garlic. In this recipe, I tried to replicate some of the most unique qualities of Mexican chocolate, using almond flour for a grainier texture, cinnamon in enough quantity that it can't be missed, and smoky ancho chili powder made from ground, dried poblano peppers to intensify the region's unique flavor profile. The ancho chili powder is a key ingredient here, so plan ahead to make sure you have it on hand before you begin. This treat is a great choice for those avoiding gluten.

It's crucial that these brownies don't get overbaked, as they can quickly become dry and crumbly. Rather have them undercooked and fudgy! To create even more intense flavor, try frosting with Espresso Icing.

BROWNIES
5 oz. unsweetened baking chocolate*
10 Tbsp. unsalted butter
2 tsp. best quality vanilla extract (I use Bourbon)
1½ tsp. ground cinnamon (I use Vietnamese)
½ tsp. ancho chili powder
4 eggs
½ tsp. kosher salt or sea salt
¾ c. raw or turbinado granulated sugar
1 c. brown sugar, packed
1 c. almond flour (leveled with a knife)
2 Tbsp. cornstarch, sifted

Preheat oven to 400 degrees. Line 8 x 8-inch square pan with parchment paper. Butter bottom and sides.

Melt unsweetened chocolate with butter in a small saucepan over low heat, stirring constantly until the mixture is smooth and glossy. If using a microwave, stop to stir every 30 seconds so the chocolate doesn't burn. Remove from heat and stir in the vanilla, cinnamon and ancho chili powder. Set aside.

*If you don't have unsweetened baking chocolate, an easy substitute is 1 Tbsp. vegetable oil and 3 Tbsp. good quality cocoa powder for every ounce of chocolate. Sift cocoa over oil and stir together until completely smooth, then melt butter and add along with flavorings as above, stirring well to combine.

Combine eggs and salt with an electric mixer. Add the sugars and beat on high for about 10 minutes, until the mixture has turned very light and thick and has doubled or tripled in volume. Add the chocolate mixture to the eggs, beating on low until just mixed. Stir in almond flour and cornstarch until integrated.

Pour the batter into the prepared pan, place in the middle of the oven, and immediately turn the temperature down to 350 degrees. Bake for 30-40 minutes; the brownies will be quite fudgy and a tester should come out with a smudge of chocolate. They will be very dark and moist. Cool completely in pan, then sprinkle with confectioners' sugar or spread with espresso icing.

ESPRESSO ICING
2 c. confectioners' sugar
¼ tsp. salt
1 Tbsp. espresso powder
1 Tbsp. hot water

Place confectioners' sugar in a bowl with salt. Dissolve espresso powder completely in hot water. Pour into bowl of sugar a little at a time, whisking until desired consistency is reached (thick but still fluid). Spread over brownies and allow to harden for half an hour before serving.

If you want to get really fancy, drizzle only half the icing going in one direction across the pan, and then add almond milk or half and half to lighten the rest, drizzling it in a crisscross pattern for contrast. When icing hardens, lift the brownies out of the pan by pulling up on the parchment paper. Set on a cutting board and cut into small squares or rectangles. *Makes about 20 to 24 small, rich brownies.*

JAKE'S HANDS-DOWN FAVORITE WARM BROWNIE PUDDING WITH RASPBERRY SAUCE

When I asked my older son, Jake, as I did with all of my kids, to name some favorite dishes for this cookbook, brownie pudding was the only thing on his list! Jake has never been very specific about his food preferences—he just knows that when he's hungry, he's *hungry*. And when brownie pudding is on the menu, he's all over it.

Despite its similar name, this dessert is nothing like a bread pudding (see Chocolate Challah Bread Pudding for more on this); it is more like a cross between a lava cake and homemade fudge. As it sounds, it's very intense, and a key to this recipe is the sweet-tart, bright magenta raspberry sauce that provides a counterpoint to the pudding's heavy, deep chocolate, taking an already-wonderful dessert to a different level altogether; I also recommend a dollop of whipped cream on top, for temperature contrast and to give taste buds a break from the intensity of the other two flavors. The raspberry sauce can, of course, be made with fresh berries, but it is absolutely fine with frozen—and in a pinch, could even be made by melting some raspberry fruit spread and omitting the sugar in the recipe (adding more hot water as needed). The brownie pudding must be served warm, and can easily be reheated, so you can make it ahead and then just put the pudding in a low oven as you are sitting down for dinner, and warm the raspberry sauce on the stove at the lowest setting as the dishes are being cleared.

Though brownie pudding is a relatively homey dessert (no fancy icings or complex pastries here) and is baked and served in a casserole dish, it can be relied upon to create a sensation every time.

BROWNIE PUDDING
4 large eggs, beaten lightly
2 c. raw sugar
½ c. unbleached all-purpose flour
¾ c. unsweetened cocoa, sifted
1 c. butter (or margarine), melted
2 tsp. vanilla extract
½ tsp. salt

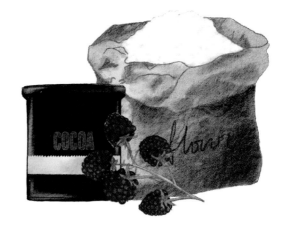

Preheat oven to 325 degrees. Grease an 8 x 8-inch square or medium round baking dish. Set aside a shallow, larger roasting pan (that the baking dish can fit into) to use as a water bath. Set a full kettle to boil.

In a large mixing bowl with electric mixer, beat eggs and sugar until very light and tripled in volume, about 5 minutes. Add flour and cocoa, mixing on low speed until blended. Mix in melted butter or margarine, vanilla, and salt on low speed. Pour batter into prepared baking dish and place inside roasting pan in the oven. Carefully pour enough hot water into larger pan to come halfway up the sides of the pudding dish. Bake for 50 to 60 minutes, until top is crusty and tester inserted ½ inch from edge comes out with no raw batter but a fudgy crumb clinging to it. Make whipped cream and raspberry sauce while pudding bakes.

WHIPPED CREAM
Pint of heavy cream
1 to 2 Tbsp. sugar

Whip cream with sugar at high speed until just stiff. Store in fridge, covered, until ready to serve.

RASPBERRY SAUCE
24 oz. frozen raspberries, or 2 pints fresh
¼ c. boiling water
½ c. raw sugar, or less to taste

Place raspberries, boiling water, and sugar in small saucepan and bring to a boil, being careful not to let it boil over (it's messy). Lower heat to simmer for 20 to 30 minutes until sauce is slightly thickened and reduced by at least a third. Keep an eye on it so it doesn't burn. Cool sauce and pour through a sieve, pressing down with a large spoon so all of the sauce moves through without the seeds, and carefully scraping the underside of the sieve with the spoon so you don't lose any of the good stuff. This is a bit labor intensive, but worthwhile, as you get a smooth, thick sauce when done. If not serving immediately, store in saucepan with lid for easy reheating.

If not eating brownie pudding the day you make it, I recommend you reheat it before serving (it's dense, so it will take about an hour at 200 degrees to get warm). Serve in bowls, topped with cool whipped cream and drizzled with warm raspberry sauce. Splendid! *Serves about 10 to 12.*

TORTA CAPRESE

This recipe, along with the one for Pasta al Limone, was given to me by the chef at Hotel La Minerva on the island of Capri in southern Italy. This *torta* (whose name means "Torte of Capri") was served to us in the mornings alongside dark cups of cappuccino or espresso, on a terrace overlooking a verdant and rugged landscape with the sea sparkling below. Capri is one of the most beautiful places I have ever seen, and I was lucky to find this little, out-of-the-way family inn, graced with loggias, vividly tiled floors, and private balconies among the citrus trees. There, it was easy to believe that the whole world was made up of warm lemon sun, beguiling green sea, and heavenly blue sky. I was thrilled that the chef was willing to share some recipes with me so I could bring back the flavors, scents, and colors of that time.

It happens that this *torta* also carries a second special association for me: I made it for my parents' 63rd anniversary party, their last before my Poppi died. His love for dark chocolate was absolute and enduring, as was his love for my mother.

Like my Marzipan Almond Torte (see next recipe), this *torta* uses almonds instead of wheat flour for its base, and it's the eggs that give it lift, which is why they must each be beaten individually as they are added. If you take your time to do that, it bakes up surprisingly high and fluffy.

I have tweaked the original recipe just a little, as I have a tendency to do. The chef calls for chopped almonds, but I like the texture better when they are ground. I suggest you try it both ways and see what you like best! I have also added a teaspoon of almond extract, which greatly increases the intensity of the almond flavor. Again, feel free to leave it out or play with your own variations.

I have converted the chef's grams to cups and teaspoons, but I have faithfully reproduced the directions in his words, adding my embellishments in brackets. The recipe itself is quite simple; the result is rich, buttery, and fragrant. *Serves about 8 to 10.*

10 Tbsp. butter, softened
1 c. raw sugar
6 eggs
2 c. ground or chopped almonds
6 oz. dark chocolate (60% to 75% cacao), chopped
1 shot glass of Disaronno or Grand Marnier, optional
¼ tsp. salt
1 tsp. almond extract
Powdered sugar for topping

Here are the exact directions given to me by the chef at La Minerva, with my embellishments in brackets:

[Preheat oven to 350 degrees.]

"In a bowl, mix the sugar and butter in little pieces (after having left out of the refrigerator for a half-hour) until you have achieved a creamy mixture [cream butter and sugar with an electric mixer]. **Add the eggs, one at a time, until each one is completely absorbed in the mixture** [leave the beater running the whole time you are adding eggs]. **Then add the almonds, chocolate, both chopped** [or ground almonds, if you like]. **Mix from the bottom to the top. Add the liquor** [and salt and extract]. **Mix again. Butter a pie pan** [cake pan] **of a diameter of about 25 cm** [9 in.], **add oven paper** [parchment] **and butter that too and** [then] **add the mixture. Put it in a preheated oven at 180 degrees** [350 F] **for forty-five minutes (time may vary according to the oven).** [Begin checking at 40 minutes; done when tester comes out with moist crumb but no wet batter.] **Take it out of the oven, let it sit** [until completely cooled] **and sprinkle with powdered sugar."**

MARZIPAN ALMOND TORTE

Marzipan is a paste of almonds and sugar that is used to make all sorts of confections. One of my happiest childhood memories is receiving a tiny basket of miniature marzipan fruits as a gift from one of my Swiss friends; aside from their Technicolor hue, these treats were made to look quite real, right down to the little green fruit basket they came in, as if they had been plucked off the grocery shelf.

Marzipan and almond paste in the US are often sold side-by-side in the baking aisle in small tubes, but almond paste seems to be easier to find. The main difference between them is that marzipan is smoother and contains more sugar—but for the purposes of this cake, if you are having difficulty finding marzipan, almond paste will do just fine.

This is a gluten-free and grain-free cake, light and airy, and quite cakey in consistency, though short in stature. In other words, it is not a tall, stately cake, but it is very satisfying. It does not taste heavily of almonds unless almond extract is added, so it can be used as a vehicle for any combination of flavors you like. I have made some suggestions below, but the possibilities are endless.

I don't only make this torte when a grain-free dessert is needed; sometimes I just want a good, moist cake without the heaviness of wheat flour. And for me, there is nothing like that marzipan blast from the past. *Serves about 8 to 10.*

For a simpler but related recipe, see Torta Caprese (previous page).

There are many options for making this torte: as below, the base can be made with citrus and/or almond flavoring, a bit of cardamom can be added for a lovely fragrance, or these can all be left out for a plainer preparation; the recipe can also be doubled to create layers for filling. The top can be dusted with confectioners' sugar, iced gently with a plain citrus or dark chocolate orange glaze (my favorite), frosted with orange buttercream, or all of the above, perfect for a celebration: doubled and filled with orange buttercream, then topped with dark chocolate orange glaze.

1 stick (8 Tbsp.) unsalted butter, softened
2 Tbsp. orange or mandarin zest, optional
½ c. raw sugar, divided
3 Tbsp. marzipan or almond paste, softened
4 large eggs, separated, room temperature
1½ c. finely ground, blanched almond flour
1 tsp. baking powder
¼ tsp. ground cardamom, optional
½ tsp. salt
1 tsp. white or cider vinegar
1 tsp. orange extract, optional (or vanilla)
1 tsp. almond extract, optional (or vanilla)

Preheat oven to 350 degrees. Prepare 8-inch nonstick springform pan: cut a circle of parchment paper for the bottom of the pan, then butter sides of pan liberally. Place butter on counter to soften. Knead marzipan with hands to soften and make easier to integrate into batter.

Zest orange or mandarin (if using) and blend in bowl of food processor with ¼ c. sugar for 1 to 2 minutes, until citrus binds with sugar (or use fingers). With an electric mixer on medium, cream citrus sugar together with butter and marzipan until light and fluffy. Separate eggs, and add yolks one at a time, beating to incorporate. (For instructions on how to separate eggs, see Sublime Chocolate Mousse.) Add almond flour, baking powder, cardamom, and salt to mixture, beating on low until it resembles moist paste.

Place egg whites in a separate mixing bowl and beat with an electric mixer on high speed. When soft peaks begin to form, add vinegar and extracts of choice while continuing to beat. Add remaining ¼ c. sugar, a little at a time, beating until egg whites are glossy and stiff.

Combine egg white mixture with almond batter, folding slowly and steadily with a rubber spatula until mixture is all one pale, golden color. Egg whites will collapse a little, but that's okay. Be as gentle as you can; they will rise again as they bake.

Bake in center of oven for 22 to 25 minutes, or until tester inserted in center comes out with a moist crumb. Do not overbake. Allow to cool to room temperature before releasing sides of pan. The torte might fall a bit in the center, but as long as it's moist, it will taste perfect. See below for topping variations.

SIMPLE TOPPING

Sift **confectioners' sugar** over top of completely cooled torte; serve with whipped cream or ice cream and fresh berries.

DARK CHOCOLATE ORANGE GLAZE

Melt ½ **c. dark chocolate chips or 3-ounce dark chocolate bar** with **1 Tbsp. butter**. Add ½ **tsp. orange extract** and **pinch salt**, and whisk until glossy. If mixture seizes, whisk in **1 or 2 Tbsp. boiling water to loosen** before spreading on completely cooled torte. Allow to set for ½ hour before serving. For a non-citrus chocolate glaze, add vanilla or almond extract instead.

ORANGE OR LEMON GLAZE

Sift **1 c. confectioners' sugar** over juice of **1 lemon**. Add ½ **tsp. lemon or orange extract**, and **pinch of salt**. Whisk until runny but still thick, adjusting proportions as needed. Pour over completely cooled torte in whatever pattern you like, allowing 30 to 60 minutes for glaze to set before serving.

ORANGE BUTTERCREAM

Cream **1 stick softened butter** with 2½ **c. confectioners' sugar** and **1 tsp. orange extract**. Add ¼ **tsp. salt** to mixture while beating on medium speed. Add **1 tsp. citrus juice** at a time (orange, tangerine, or tart orange) until desired thickness is reached and frosting is smooth and creamy. Spread on completely cooled torte and garnish with dried mandarins or orange slices if desired.

For celebration layer cake: Double torte recipe and divide batter, baking in two pans according to instructions. When torte is completely cooled, remove one torte from pan, peel off parchment, and place on cake plate. Frost with orange buttercream, carefully placing second torte layer on top. Prepare dark chocolate orange glaze as above, and cover top and sides of torte, decorating as desired.

CHOCOLATE CHALLAH BREAD PUDDING WITH VANILLA BOURBON SAUCE

It seems fitting that I have started and ended this book with challah, given the multitude of meals that we have begun—and I hope will continue to begin—by breaking bread together. I know it's not always possible to make a big, complicated meal, but home cooking of any kind has a way of bringing the household to the table. If we can set aside our phones, our little hurts, our tasks that we think are too important to wait, and gather around once a day, then we will always stay connected, however imperfectly. Like our human connections, cooking is not meant to be perfect, and it's not always easy; but we all need to eat, right? It's simply the best thing we can do as a family, as a community: to prepare nourishing food for each other and—with a bit of time and good fortune—sit down and enjoy it together.

This recipe is good for a crowd, and it's not nearly as complex as it looks. I used to make it for family brunches and annual holiday parties, and Gabriella recently made it to break a Yom Kippur fast. Think of the bread pudding as a form of French toast, and prepare the sauce while the pudding is in the oven. This pudding doesn't even need a water bath! It's unnecessary to make this dish with a homemade challah (unless it's gone quite stale, which is unlikely to ever happen if your family is anything like mine); your efforts will be obscured in the pudding. Just buy a nice, eggy challah or brioche for the purpose.

BREAD PUDDING
1 whole challah (or brioche)
2 c. whole milk
¼ c. melted butter
¼ c. raw sugar
½ tsp. salt
4 eggs, pref. free range, beaten
1 tsp. vanilla extract
2 c. grated dark chocolate (60% cacao)

Preheat oven to 350 degrees. Cut challah into chunks and place in a large, wide mixing bowl. In a second bowl, combine milk, melted butter, sugar, and salt, whisking until well combined. Add eggs and vanilla, whisking again to integrate. Pour milk mixture over challah chunks and use hands to toss until all are coated with liquid and the structure of the challah is beginning to collapse a bit.

Shave chocolate on large side of grater, and stir thoroughly into wet challah mixture. Spoon all into a large, buttered dish (at least 9 x 13 inches, preferably with a deep bottom), leveling top. Bake in center of oven for 45 to 60 minutes, removing when pudding has begun to steam and protruding edges of challah are beginning to look crisp. Make sauce while pudding bakes.

VANILLA BOURBON SAUCE
¼ c. butter
2 Tbsp. white flour or 1 Tbsp. cornstarch
2 to 4 Tbsp. raw sugar (to taste)
1 tsp. quality vanilla extract
1 c. heavy cream
¼ tsp. salt
¼ c. bourbon or other whiskey

Melt butter in medium saucepan, and add flour or cornstarch, whisking continuously to create a roux (smooth paste). In a separate bowl or large measuring cup, combine sugar, vanilla, cream, and salt, then add this mixture to roux, whisking constantly until they blend together with no lumps. Whisk in bourbon. Heat mixture on medium-high just until it begins to bubble, whisking or stirring almost constantly so it doesn't burn. If lumps form, whisk in a bit more cream; if this fails, push the sauce through a sieve. If sauce gets too thick, again whisk in a bit of milk or cream. Sauce should be smooth and pourable.

Serve warm bread pudding drizzled with warm vanilla bourbon sauce, bringing the extra to the table in a creamer for guests who will inevitably want more.

If you are making this pudding ahead to serve on a later day, you will need time to rewarm it (it is meant to be served warm). It is dense and will retain the cold for a long time. Take pan out and leave it on the counter for a couple of hours, then reheat at 200 degrees for at least an hour. Re-warm sauce at very low heat to avoid burning, whisking in a bit more cream if needed. See next page for variations. *Serves 8 to 10.*

BREAD PUDDING VARIATIONS

There are a great number of possible variations for this bread pudding, accomplished either by adding flavors to the chocolate mixture or by changing the base flavors. For a mocha variation, add **a shot or two of espresso** and **an extra Tbsp. sugar** to the challah when you're soaking it. To make a Mexican hot chocolate bread pudding, mix in **1 Tbsp. of cinnamon and 1 tsp. ancho chili powder** with chocolate.

Or try making a fruit-based pudding using berries or stone fruits, and adjust the sauce as needed. Here are two fruit variations that have gone over exceptionally well in our house:

APPLE CINNAMON BREAD PUDDING

Eliminate chocolate from pudding. Add **4 peeled and diced apples** tossed with **1 tsp. cinnamon and 2 Tbsp. sugar**. If you like, add **1. c. dried cranberries** to the mixture. Bake pudding for a full hour to cook the fruit. For the sauce, add **1 tsp. of cinnamon to the vanilla bourbon mixture if desired**, or make a quick salted caramel sauce instead, by warming **1 c. prepared salted caramel sauce and whisking with ¼ c. cream**.

PEACHES AND CREAM BREAD PUDDING

Eliminate chocolate from pudding. Add 4 peeled and diced peaches (can use frozen and thawed peaches if peaches are not in season) tossed with **2 Tbsp. sugar** (if needed) **or 2 Tbsp. peach schnapps**, if you're feeling saucy. **Replace ½ c. of the milk with heavy cream** to intensify the "peaches and cream" effect. Also delicious is **a generous sprinkling of nuts on the top—almonds, pistachios, walnuts, or pecans** go well. Bake pudding for a full hour since the fruit will need time to cook. The vanilla bourbon sauce goes beautifully with peaches.

ACKNOWLEDGEMENTS

I am so very grateful to those who took time to read this cookbook in progress: my dear, brilliant friends, Miranda Volpe, Lynn Nevins, and Jeremy Warner. Your keen input and enthusiasm bolstered my clarity and sense of purpose.

I am greatly indebted to Roman Kostovski for his formatting, design, and publishing assistance, and his calm during our myriad technical malfunctions.

Many thanks to my loving children: Gabriella, for providing the impetus, editing, and gorgeous website for this book; Louis, for recognizing that cooking is a love language, and for finding Gaby so you could both give us Asher; Jake, for photo editing, feedback, and reminding us that ten thousand hours is just the beginning; Mayu, for showing us how to run a business with class and for your wonder at everything I cook; Jesse, for your recipes, proofreading, indexing, and a million moments of joy in the kitchen; and Serena, for your artistic vision and dogged persistence.

I owe an exceptional debt of gratitude to Serena, who spent an untold amount of time at this labor of love, drawing away in her studio until the wee hours or squeezed side-by-side with me at my desk while she read, considered, guided, revised, laughed, shouted, dragged, untangled—and above all, blessed these pages with her glorious works of art. Bean, you have given wings to my words.

Finally, I am thankful for the privilege and good fortune that have made possible this life full of cooking, writing, and walking by the sea.

ABOUT THE AUTHOR

RACHEL MIRANDA is a freelance writer and editor of cultural, literary, and academic works, and the managing editor of Plamen Press. She specializes in editing translations, and was the recipient of a 2017 Literature Translation Fellowship from the National Endowment for the Arts. She has an MFA in Writing and Literature from the Bennington Writing Seminars and a BA in European Cultural Studies from Brandeis University. She currently makes her home in Connecticut, near her dear family and a small cove of the Long Island Sound, where she continues her lifelong practices of cooking, baking, and writing. This is her first published book.

ABOUT THE ARTIST

SERENA FAYE FEINGOLD is a community artist, illustrator, and object maker whose work centers around visual storytelling. She received a BFA from the School of the Museum of Fine Arts at Tufts University, and a certification in Majolica glazing from the Scuola d'Arte Ceramica Romano Ranieri in Deruta, Italy. In 2017, she completed a residency at the Skopelos Foundation in Skopelos, Greece. Feingold is currently living in Connecticut, where she teaches pottery and runs her jewelry, illustration, and ceramics business, Bina.

INDEX

C